TEACHING for RESULTS

TEACHING
FOR
RESULTS

Findley B. Edge

BROADMAN PRESS
Nashville, Tennessee

© 1956 • BROADMAN PRESS
Nashville, Tennessee

All rights reserved.
International copyright secured.

4234-01
ISBN: 0-8054-3401-1

PRINTED IN THE UNITED STATES OF AMERICA

To
My Wife
LOUVENIA LITTLETON EDGE

PREFACE

The improvement of teaching in the Sunday school is one of the most pressing problems facing our churches today. This is not to minimize nor depreciate the type of teaching that is being done at the present time. Our teachers, themselves, are the ones most keenly aware of their own limitations and are the most urgent in their request for guidance and help. Unfortunately, the title of this book promises more than it is able to deliver. It points to an objective to be sought rather than assuring means of accomplishment. Yet it is hoped that some of the ideas and suggestions presented will be helpful to teachers in achieving better results from their teaching.

The Sunday school has become an important and integral part of the life of our churches. It is one of the most powerful forces for good in modern society. In churches of various sizes and types all over this land, teachers lead children, young people, and adults in a study of the Bible, seeking together to understand its meaning and significance for Christian living. In spite of weaknesses and difficulties, God has used the efforts of devoted teachers to accomplish often significant results in the lives of those whom they teach.

On the other hand, the teachers are the ones who most often are aware of the fact that they are not getting the results they desire—either in Bible knowledge or in Christian living. In spite of the fact that some members have attended Sunday school for five, ten, fifteen, or more years, there is an amazing lack of Bible knowledge even among those who are

most regular in attendance. This is a matter of no little significance, for although the quality and depth of one's spiritual life is not necessarily conditioned by his knowledge of the
Bible, this knowledge does contribute to a more intelligent
faith. The problem of securing results in Christian living is
even more serious.

It is our belief that one of the reasons we have not been
able to achieve desired results is that our aims, and therefore
our teaching, have not been sufficiently specific. Teachers
have been guided by aims that were general and often vague.
As a result, members have not seen the relevance to their
own experience of what was taught. Thus, the Sunday school
class has tended to become a place where high Christian ideals
are discussed. Too often this study ends only in discussion
without sufficient carry-over into daily life in the home, school,
business, recreational activities, social activities, and other
areas of experience.

In general, the objectives Christian teachers seek may be
subsumed under three headings: knowledge, inspiration, and
conduct response. A knowledge aim is one in which the
teacher desires to lead the group in a systematic study of a
portion of the Bible leading to an understanding of the
meaning of the Bible and a mastery of the facts involved. In
an inspiration aim, the teacher seeks to lead the class in a
study and acceptance of a general Christian ideal or attitude.
In a conduct response aim, the teacher seeks to lead the class
to express some Christian ideal or attitude in terms of specific responses in their everyday relationships. Much confusion and vagueness have come in teaching because teachers
have sought to achieve all three of these objectives at the same
time, with the result that none of them were adequately
achieved. While these aims are certainly not mutually exclusive, it is the thesis of this book that greater results will be
obtained if the teacher, in a given lesson or series of lessons,
will identify the type of aim he desires and then work toward
that with a singleness of purpose.

Thus, one of the first tasks of the teacher as he begins his lesson preparation is to determine, in light of the lesson or lessons to be taught and in light of the needs of the class, which type of aim he desires to achieve. Does he wish to help his class members secure an understanding of the meaning of the Bible and some mastery of the facts involved? Of course, some inspiration may attend this study, and some conduct response may result in the lives of the members. If so, fine. But from the viewpoint of the teacher in this lesson or series of lessons the dominant purpose is to lead the class to an understanding of meaning and to some mastery of facts. Therefore everything that is done—the materials selected, the content studied, the methods used—is designed with knowledge as the dominant objective.

Or, does the teacher desire to lead the group to an understanding and acceptance of a general Christian attitude? If so, inspiration will be his primary aim. Or, does he desire a specific conduct response? Obviously, this response will have to be based on a knowledge of the meaning of the Bible and an understanding and acceptance of some general Christian attitudes; but these—knowledge and inspiration—are means, not ends, in this particular lesson. They are instrumental to the achieving of the conduct response. In this type of lesson, everything that is done will be determined by the conduct response sought.

All three of these objectives—knowledge, inspiration, and conduct response—are worthy. The Christian teacher will strive for now one, now the other. However, in this book we are emphasizing only the approach to be followed in seeking a conduct response aim. We have chosen to follow this emphasis because we believe Christian living is the ultimate objective of all Christian teaching. The chapters 6–11, dealing with the various divisions of a lesson plan, all present the approach that may be taken to achieve a conduct response aim. In no way is this emphasis intended to minimize the value of the knowledge aim and the inspiration aim. They, too, have their significant place in any total view of Christian teaching.

The principles presented here are not just theory. They have been used with teachers in numerous churches and have been discussed with hundreds of teachers in other churches over the South—in state teaching clinics, and in Southwide assemblies. The enthusiastic response of these teachers to the ideas presented encouraged me to believe that they may be helpful to others.

An attempt has been made to make this book as practical as possible by giving numerous illustrations and examples of the principles that are discussed. It is written in non-technical language to be more easily used by the serious Sunday school teacher who is seeking help. It may also be useful to pastors, ministers of education, and any others who have responsibility for teacher-training in the local church. In chapter 14 a plan is suggested whereby the weekly officers and teachers' meeting may be used as a continuous school for teacher improvement. This book could certainly be the basis for such a study. It may also be resource material for the person who is leading a group of teachers in a study of one of the books in the regular Training Course Series. It is designed to be sufficiently comprehensive in scope for use in colleges and seminaries in courses dealing with principles of teaching in the Sunday school.

I would like to acknowledge my indebtedness to Dr. Gaines S. Dobbins, Dean of the School of Religious Education, Southern Baptist Seminary, who first introduced me to the whole field of religious education and who, by his own peerless teaching, kindled within me an interest in this area that has deepened with the passing of the years. I would also like to express my appreciation to my colleagues, Dr. Sabin Landry and Mr. Ernest Loessner, and to a former colleague, Dr. Denton Coker, who in many conversations helped me to clarify the ideas and suggestions given here. For reading the manuscript and for making numerous constructive criticisms,

I am indebted to Dr. Coker, now Assistant Professor of Religious Education, Southeastern Baptist Seminary, Dr. J. M. Price, Director of the School of Religious Education, Southwestern Baptist Seminary, and Dr. Paul H. Vieth, Horace Bushnell Professor of Christian Nurture, Yale University Divinity School. Miss Clara McCartt and Mrs. Frances Duvall rendered invaluable assistance both in typing the manuscript and in making suggestions concerning matters of style. And last, but by no means least, I want to express appreciation to my wife and to my two boys, Larry and Hoyt, for their continuing interest and encouragement.

FINDLEY B. EDGE

CONTENTS

xiii

I

JESUS CAME TEACHING

Into the midst of the encrusted formalism of Judaism Jesus came, lived, and taught. His matchless message and dynamic teaching burst through the hard crust of the religious traditionalism that had engulfed the Jewish people and fanned the smoldering ember of their faith until it became a living fire. How did he do it? Volumes have been written and could be written in answer to this question. However, a part of the answer must be found in the content and the manner of his masterful teaching. Here, as elsewhere, Jesus becomes both our Teacher and our Example.

In thinking of the kind of teaching that will secure results, we, as Christian teachers, go back to the divine Teacher for our inspiration, for our content, for valid motivation for Christian action, and for proper principles and methods of achieving the results. Others have presented Jesus as the master Teacher.[1] They have indicated his interest in and concern for persons; they have identified the principles of teaching and learning which he observed; they have evaluated the methods he used. Little would be gained by restating these findings. Rather, it is our purpose here to analyze and evaluate the educational principles followed by Jesus in light of Jewish education that was current in his day. It is important for us to know not only what he taught and how he taught but also what he rejected. It may be that through such an

[1] Horne, H. H., *Jesus the Master Teacher* (New York: Association Press, 1920); Price, J. M., *Jesus the Teacher* (Nashville: The Sunday School Board of the Southern Baptist Convention, 1946); Weigle, L. A., *Jesus and the Educational Method* (New York: The Abingdon Press, 1939); McKay, C. F., *The Art of Jesus as Teacher* (Philadelphia: The Judson Press, 1930).

1

analysis we may find that in our teaching today we have fallen into some of the practices against which he reacted and which he rejected.

Throughout this volume we will be emphasizing the importance of securing results through our teaching. But we do not want results "at any price." We must be careful to seek only those that are the free outward manifestation of an inner relationship of the individual with God. With this principle probably all will agree. The achieving of this principle is neither as easy nor as simple as it may appear on the surface. The experience of Jesus with the scribes and the Pharisees will serve to illustrate the problem we face and to indicate some of the danger points we must avoid.

JESUS AND THE SYNAGOGUE

In the time of Jesus the strategic importance of the synagogue for both religious and educational purposes can hardly be overestimated. It was the nerve center of Judaism. Here the people learned the rituals, ceremonies, fasts, and other obligations that were supposed to be followed under the law. The synagogue was the real dynamic in the formation and expression of Judaism. Outside of Jerusalem, particularly, it had come to supercede the Temple in the hearts of the people and in its influence on their lives. Synagogues were found in almost every town and village in Palestine. They were truly the schools of the people.

Throughout his life and ministry Jesus was rather closely associated with the synagogue. Undoubtedly it was here, as well as in his home, that he received much of his early religious training. It was his custom to attend the meetings in the synagogue (Luke 4:16; Mark 1:29), and it was there that he made his first specific statement of his life's purpose as he began his public ministry (Luke 4:18–27). Throughout his ministry he often taught in the synagogue (Matt. 13:54; John 6:59; John 18:20).

Although Jesus did not break with the synagogue as an

educational institution, he did break with the traditional, authoritative, transmissive education that was carried on there. As the old system of Judaism could not contain the spiritual dynamic of his teachings, so the Jewish educational system could not contain his new approach to teaching. He broke with the type of education that had to appeal to ancient authorities to be accepted or believed. The formula found on almost every page of the Talmud, "Rabbi A. says that Rabbi B. says," or "Rabbi C. says in the name of Rabbi D.," is lacking in Jesus' teachings. He dared to say, "Ye have heard that it was said by them of old time, . . . but I say unto you" (Matt. 5:21–22). When he finished the Sermon on the Mount, the multitudes were astonished, "For he taught them as one having authority and not as one of their scribes" (Matt. 7:28–29). The authority of the latter was external and second-hand; his authority was intrinsic, fresh, and free.

Wherein lay the source of Jesus' authority? He was divine as well as human. He was the speaker for God. One who is that, even in a lesser way, always speaks with authority. A part of the convincing evidence of his authority was in his penetrating insight into the meaning and message of the Old Testament Scriptures. A part of it was in the reasonableness and the profound simplicity of what he taught as he dealt with the basic truths of God, man, and the universe. It was in his evident sincerity as well as in his manner and method of teaching. Certainly, a part of it was found in the life he lived. For his life not only lent power to his teaching but provided a concrete illustration of what he taught. One will search long and far to find a greater authority than this.

JESUS AND THE SCRIPTURES

Jesus had the highest regard for the ancient Scriptures. From earliest childhood he had studied them. They had become a part of his knowledge and his experience. His familiarity with them is evidenced by his numerous references to the Old Testament. However, Jesus refused to follow the current transmissive method of teaching them. In his day, Jewish education consisted mainly in memorizing portions of the Scriptures and in learning the traditional interpretations contained in the oral law. As important and necessary as the transmission of the facts and knowledge is, Jesus recognized that this was not all that was necessary. The danger of a transmissive type of education is that the individual may learn facts about religion without experiencing them. Therefore, education under Jesus did not consist in memorizing a code of ethics he worked out for his followers. Rather, he encouraged and stimulated his disciples to think for themselves. He developed in his followers the ability to solve problems which life presented.

At the present time, there seems to be a trend in religious education back to an emphasis on the content and message of the Bible.[2] This trend is altogether wholesome and much needed in light of the emphasis we have had on "present experience" which was often devoid of any content. However, lest we get the idea that a "return to the Bible" or an "emphasis on content" will be the panacea for all our ills in religious education, let us be reminded that there is more to the task of Christian teaching than an emphasis on content or even an emphasis on practice. It would be difficult indeed to find a period in religious history when a greater emphasis was placed on both a knowledge and practice of the Law than was done by the Pharisees in the time of Jesus.

The following quotations from *The Mishna* will serve to show the esteem in which a knowledge of the Law was held:

When a scholar of the wise sits and studies and forgets a word of his Mishna, they account it to him as worthy of death.
    The more study of the Law the more life: . . . if he has gained for himself words of the Law he has gained for himself life in the world to come.
    These are things whose fruits a man enjoys in this world while the capital is laid up for him in the world to come; honoring

[2] Cf. Smart, James D., *The Teaching Ministry of the Church* (Philadelphia: The Westminster Press, 1954).

father and mother, deeds of loving-kindness, making peace between a man and his fellow; and the study of the Law is equal to them all.

Thus, all zeal for education aimed at making the whole people a people of the Law. When the child was taught how to read, it was the text of the Scriptures that he read. In reality it was the interest in the Law which made reading rather widely diffused at this time.

Jewish religious education emphasized, even demanded, practice of the Law as well as a mastery of its content. No one could accuse the average Jew, and certainly not the Pharisee, of any lack of observance of the religious requirements. While this was a worthy objective, unfortunately it seems that a mere outward conformity to the Law became the chief aim of legalistic Judaism. Both the emphasis and the method of education were at fault. In too many instances it was practice without proper motivation and observance without spirit. In the *Halakhah* every legal ordinance was indicated in the most minute detail as to outward observances, "but beyond this it left the inner man, the spring of action, untouched." [3] The duty of the Jew was to follow the letter of the commands as given. Whether he submitted to the Law willingly or grudgingly, whether he kept the commands in the spirit of the Law or as a matter of mere form was of little consequence. The virtue and the reward were in the doing of the act itself. This conformity to an external, authoritarian, legal norm was one of the main factors in the loss of the spirit of the Law which Jesus condemned. For the orthodox Jew, there was only one duty—outward conformity to the commands of the Law and to the traditions of the scribes.

JESUS AND FREEDOM

One of the truly amazing features of the educational ministry of Jesus was the freedom which he allowed his learners

[3] Edersheim, Alfred, *The Life and Times of Jesus the Messiah* (Grand Rapids: William B. Eerdmans Publishing Co., 1942), I, 105. Used by permission.

and the freedom which he demanded for himself. As has been indicated, Jesus had the highest regard for the Old Testament Scriptures, but he had little or no regard for the casuistical laws of rabbinical interpretation. Although he based his teachings solidly within the framework of the Old Testament, he refused to be bound by the traditional interpretations that were current in his day. He rejected practically all the religious institutions upon which the pharisaical scribes placed chief emphasis: fasting, rigid Sabbath observance, and the laws of ceremonial cleanliness. Judged by the standards of his day, Jesus was unorthodox both in what he taught and in the method by which he taught.

The education of this period was strictly traditional. It was forbidden for anyone to use individual initiative and to interpret the Scriptures contrary to tradition. To do so meant that the individual would be "put out of the temple," or excommunicated. The privilege of the individual to find the spirit of the Law for himself in his own experience was taken from him, and in its place he was given a set of traditional laws that demanded only outward conformity.

Before we become overly-critical, we must remind ourselves that it was not with any malicious intent that this freedom was taken from the masses of the people. It is almost certain that this practice came from a sincere desire to guard them from error. The leaders of Judaism felt that only those who were carefully trained in the study of the Law were qualified to interpret it for the people. Their reasoning was that since their interpretation of truth was perfect and complete then anything they could do to keep the masses from coming to conclusions which were contrary to their interpretation was not only justifiable but necessary, even to the point of compulsion. Furthermore, if salvation was found only within the sphere of their interpretation of truth and if damnation was outside this interpretation, then anything they could do to keep the individual from going outside of "truth," whether it be by an authoritative type of teaching or by some other form of compulsion, was beneficial to the individual for it saved him from damnation. Herein is found one of the differences between those who believe in the authority of the church and those who believe in individual freedom. But however benevolent the intent, the fact is, freedom was taken from the people.

There are many evidences that the Jew, during the earthly ministry of Jesus, had become subject to an external authority. The oral law came to have a place of power even above that occupied by the written Law. These traditional interpretations of the scribes were more authoritative and binding than the written Law itself. As A. T. Robertson says, "When the commandment and tradition clashed, tradition was supreme." [4] It is no wonder that Jesus vehemently charged, "Full well do ye reject the commandment of God, that ye may keep your traditions" (Mark 7:9). The oral traditions covered every area of man's life—private, family, public, and religious. They provided for every possible and improbable situation and with iron logic and minute analysis pursued and dominated man, laying upon him a yoke that was unbearable. Nothing was left to individual initiative or conscience.

This type of education preserved orthodoxy, but it lost spiritual meaning. The value of preserving their orthodoxy as opposed to the idolatry of heathenism is not to be questioned. But, unfortunately, in their exclusive education they lost the spiritual meaning of the penetrating teachings of the prophets and fell into a cold, narrow formalism. There is no attempt here to minimize the value and importance of orthodoxy. It is basic that a person hold correct doctrines. The difficulty was that the traditional Jewish doctrines had deviated from the spirit and truth of God's revelation. In holding to their orthodox doctrines, they were thwarting both the commandments and the purposes of God.

[4] Robertson, A. T., *The Pharisees and Jesus* (New York: Charles Scribner's Sons, 1920), pp. 19-20. Used by permission.

To maintain certain doctrinal beliefs had become more important than the relieving of human suffering. Jesus confronted this problem many times in his encounter with the religious leaders. They watched him to see if he would heal a man's withered hand on the sabbath. They condemned him for healing a man born blind because it was the sabbath. The man himself they cast out of the Temple because he would not conform to their traditional interpretations. It is a travesty when orthodoxy comes to be valued above the saving of life, yet this was the situation in legalistic Judaism.

It was not so with Jesus. In an authoritarian type of education the subject matter is considered so important that independent thinking is discouraged or forbidden; passive acceptance is encouraged or demanded. In contrast, although Jesus had the most important subject matter education has ever known, the message that would lead to the establishing of right relations between man and God, he left the individual free to think for himself and to choose for himself. This of necessity must be true if religion is to be experiential. Although authoritarian education may force conformity on the part of the individual, external authority can never force belief or experiential religion upon a person. When the rich young ruler came to Jesus inquiring how he might inherit eternal life, Jesus explained the implications it would have in his personal life. The young man rejected it and went away. Jesus looked after him sorrowing, but no matter how much Jesus desired that this young man conform to his teachings, he would not force that conformity.

After the feeding of the five thousand, Jesus was perhaps at the peak of his popularity. Great multitudes followed him, and he gave the discourse which explained the spiritual nature of his kingdom. This was so out of line with Jewish expectations that many of his followers "went back, and walked no more with him" (John 6:66). Then follows Jesus' momentous question to his disciples, "Would ye also go away?" (John 6:67). Humanly speaking, the success or failure of his

mission on earth, the future of the kingdom, hinged upon
the answer of the disciples to this question, yet they had to be
left free to accept or reject, to choose for themselves. The individual must be his own final authority for religion and education to be experiential.

Jesus not only left men free to accept or reject this new relationship between man and God, but he also left man free,
after he accepted this new relationship, to work out the implications of it in his own experience. Jesus refused to work out
a detailed code of ethics which defined minutely what man
must do in every situation of life. He was content to lay
down broad principles to aid his disciples in solving their
own particular problems. He kept a careful oversight of
them, aiding them whenever necessary, but always encouraging them to think for themselves. He did not form an elabo-
rate organization to carry on his work; he simply called
twelve disciples, taught them, and left them to work out the
details for future work. He did not tell his disciples the kind
of amusements in which they might safely indulge; he told
them to strive to be like him. He did not form a detailed
creedal statement; he simply said the essence of religion was
to love God with the whole heart and one's neighbor as one-
self. This was revolutionary as contrasted with Jewish education under the scribes and Pharisees.

JESUS AND MOTIVATION

Jesus was deeply concerned with the motives of men that
lay behind and prompted outward responses. He was constantly seeking to lead individuals into a spiritual relationship with God that would express itself in outward acts. It
was the spiritual relationship that was important and not the
outward act alone.

The type of education of his day was concerned primarily
with outward acts. It taught that the observance of the ceremonial law was counted as righteousness regardless of the
motive or spirit behind it. In one of his clashes with the

scribes and Pharisees because he failed to heed their ceremonial law, Jesus said, "Go ye and learn what this meaneth,
I desire mercy and not sacrifice" (Matt. 9:13). Jesus was here
charging the revered and pious teachers of the law with ignorance of Hosea 6:6. A. T. Robertson says that "the 'Go ye
and learn' was a common formula with the rabbis, and the
use of it by Jesus as a rabbi to rabbis had additional force and
even sting." [5] One can imagine the consternation and indig-
nation of these Jewish teachers as they listened to one who
had never even attended the rabbinic schools accuse them of
ignorance of the Law that they had spent their lives studying.
But Jesus, in teaching his followers, had to change not only
the content but the method of their thinking. According to
Squires, "He led their attention away from the outward act
to the inner thought and attitude which were the source of
the outward act." [6]

This emphasis by the Jews on the outward act without sufficient concern for inner motivation led to certain unfortunate and undesirable results. For one thing, it saved a system
but lost the individual. One of the main results was the preservation of traditional Judaism. Judaism, as an institution,
was no longer a means to an end; it became an end in itself.
It was the object of supreme value, and the preservation of
the institution came to be the all-absorbing aim.

This type of education achieved an external conformity
but it lost the inner experience. In this period, religion came
to be not a communion between man and God but a "conduct legally correct." This legalistic observance cared little
for inward motive; it was concerned primarily with outward
observance. Since the motives were of an external nature, the
result was an externalizing of the religious and moral life.
When the individual became subject to an external authority, a legal norm, the result was inevitably a formal external-

[5] *Ibid.*, p. 114.
[6] Squires, W. A., *The Pedagogy of Jesus in the Twilight of Today* (New
York: George H. Doran Co., 1927), p. 127. Used by permission.

ism in life. Freedom is the essence of moral action. But when
the moral life of an individual was placed under this legal
norm, free moral action became completely crushed under
the burden of numberless legal requirements. In every area
of life, action no longer proceeded from inward motive, was
no longer the free manifestation of a moral disposition, but
resulted from the external constraint of a legal requirement.
All depended on the external correctness of the action.

Numerous evidences of formal externalism in the religious
life of the Jew in the time of Jesus and examples of how far
the spirit of the law had been lost are seen in the ingenious,
even ludicrous, ways that were devised for evading yet keeping the sabbath commandments. It was forbidden for one to
walk more than 2,000 cubits on the sabbath. This might cause
inconvenience for one who wanted to travel farther than this
on the sabbath. Thus it was "interpreted" that if he who desired to go farther than the 2,000 cubits would, before the
sabbath, place at the end of this limit food for two meals, he
could declare this to be his abode, and then he was permitted
to travel still another 2,000 cubits. Also, if one should be on
the road when the sabbath began and see at a distance of 2,000
cubits a tree or a well, he was permitted to declare this as his
sabbath abode and travel another 2,000 cubits. However, he
must observe the law according to the letter. If he said only
"Let my Sabbath resting-place be under it," that was not sufficient, for this was too indefinite and general, rather he must
say, "Let my Sabbath resting-place be at its roots" (Erubin
4:7). Schurer concludes, "Innocent as such trifling may be in
itself, it nevertheless terribly shows that the moral point of
view was entirely superceded by the legal and formal one,
that the effort was really to do justice to the letter of the law,
even though its meaning was evaded." [7]

Jesus, too, was interested in "results." On many occasions

[7] Schurer, Emil, *The Jewish People in the Time of Jesus Christ* (New
York: Charles Scribner's Sons, n.d.), Div. II, Vol. II, p. 122. Used by permission.

he emphasized the importance, even the necessity, for his followers to give an outward expression of their religion in everyday relationships. "Whosoever heareth these sayings of mine and doeth them, I will liken him unto a wise man . . ." (Matt. 7:24). "If ye love me, keep my commandments" (John 14:15). "Ye are my friends if ye do whatsoever I command you" (John 15:14). "Wherefore by their fruits ye shall know them" (Matt. 7:20). But, and here is the point we want to emphasize, Jesus sought to lead men into a relationship with God so that the "results" came as the outward expression of a life transformed by that new relationship. Herein is found both the motive and the power for any results we may seek as Christian teachers.

Obviously, the lives of all whom Jesus taught were not thus changed. But when we look at those who did enter into this new relationship with God we are impressed by the transformation in their lives and the depth of their conviction even in the face of the most serious personal and social difficulties.

Because of the masterful way in which Jesus taught, men began to live abundant lives, worthy of the God whom Jesus revealed. The test as to whether or not the teaching of Jesus was experiential is not hard to find. That his followers learned their "lessons" is proved by the way in which they were willing to live by them and die for them. The lessons they learned in the "classroom" carried over into everyday life. Their transformed lives were so fruitful and dynamic that people marveled at them (Acts 2:12). They grasped his teaching so fully in their experience and considered what they had learned to be so valuable that they felt compelled to share these teachings with others. The Book of Acts is a continuous illustration of the strong impulse to share with others the precious, life-giving knowledge they had gained, even in the face of persecution. Men do not normally suffer hardships for lessons that are only half learned, nor do they die for doctrines to which they give mere intellectual assent.

Starting from an insignificant province, from a despised race, proclaimed in the main by a mere handful of unlearned men, demanding a self-control and renunciation before unheard of, challenging everything for which the pagan world stood, undergoing almost unbelievable persecution, the Christian movement had many odds against it. However, religion was no longer a matter of intellectual assent and external obedience to a legalistic norm. Religion was now a matter of vital life experience, and neither the might of the Roman Empire nor the wiles of Satan were able to overcome it. Jesus taught, and men's attitudes were changed; their habits were changed; their lives were changed and brought in line with the will of God. This was religious education at its best. This is the kind of results that we as Christian teachers seek today.

II

EMPHASIZING RESULTS

One of the marvels of our time is the growth and success of the modern Sunday school. Using volunteer lay leadership, with limited time, often with inadequate space and equipment, the Sunday school continues to march forward. In spite of the fact that it has been soundly criticized by certain psychologists and educators, the Sunday school continues to enrich the lives of those who attend. This has been due in large measure to the fact that our churches are blessed with earnest, sincere, consecrated Christian teachers and officers. Willingly and joyfully they give of their time and energy to this tremendously important task.

WE ARE NOT GETTING THE RESULTS WE DESIRE

Yet those who work closest with the Sunday school would be the first to admit they are not getting the results they desire. Christian teachers are doing the best they know how, but they are conscious of the fact that there is urgent need for improvement.

In the area of Bible knowledge.—Arthur Flake, one of the outstanding leaders of Sunday school work of the last generation, said, "The avowed purpose of the Sunday school is to teach the Bible." This emphasis has been one of the strengths of evangelical Christianity. However, in spite of it, many people, even those who attend regularly, are woefully ignorant concerning Bible knowledge. In a nation-wide survey of Bible knowledge conducted by a leading magazine, the findings were tragic as well as revealing.[1] In this test Catholic

---

[1] *Pageant,* December, 1949, pp. 20–26. Used by permission, Hillman Periodicals, Inc.

youngsters made an average grade of 46 per cent. Protestant children made an average grade of 35 per cent. The group of individuals who did not attend Sunday school made an average grade of 30.4 per cent. They had absorbed this much religious information simply because they lived in our culture. It is a sad commentary indeed to find that Protestants made only 4.6 per cent higher grade than those who did not attend Sunday school at all. Of those tested, 73.4 per cent did not know the name of the disciple who betrayed Jesus. Seventy and .7 per cent did not know that Paul was the great apostle to the Gentiles. If there is any validity at all in this test, this surely is cause for alarm!

Another Bible knowledge test was given to approximately 18,500 high school students in the South.[2] Of this group 16,-000 could not name three prophets of the Old Testament. Twelve thousand of this high school group could not name the four Gospels. Ten thousand could not name three disciples of Jesus. A knowledge of biblical facts does not necessarily give an accurate measure of a person's spiritual development, but it is certainly a desirable objective for a Christian to be familiar with the Bible. Although teaching Bible knowledge is not the ultimate aim of the Sunday school, it is one of its important tasks. This would seem to indicate that we are not getting the results in Bible knowledge we would desire.

In the area of Christian living.—While it is true that Bible knowledge is not the primary objective of Sunday school teaching, Christian living is. A mere casual observation would indicate that we are not getting the results in changed lives we have a right to expect. Teaching does not carry over sufficiently into life. Too often it dies in the classroom. In the Great Commission Jesus said, "Go ye therefore, and teach all nations, baptizing them in the name of the Father, and of the Son and of the Holy Ghost: teaching them *to observe* all

[2] Miller, M. C., *Teaching the Multitudes* (Bridgewater: The Beacon Publishers, 1944), pp. 12–13. Used by permission.

things whatsoever I have commanded you: and, lo, I am with you alway, even unto the end of the world" (Matt. 28:19–20). Here Jesus emphasizes that our task is not just to teach men the content of his message; he indicates also that it is not completed until those whom we teach practice in their daily lives that which we teach.

TWO DANGERS TEACHERS FACE

As the teacher considers the task of trying to teach for Christian living, there are two dangers which he confronts. These come upon the teacher so subtly and their growth is so imperceptible that most teachers are not even aware of them. For this reason, they are all the more insidious.

The danger of leading the members to learn only verbalized concepts.—This is a problem that confronts any type of education, but it is a particular problem in religious education because basically Christianity is an experience—an experience with Christ that must express itself in experience. One does not truly learn a Christian ideal until he has both experienced it and expressed it in experience. Yet the teacher, in large measure, must use words in order to try to communicate this Christian experience to his class.

As the learner progresses from childhood, through youth into adulthood, teachers use words to teach him religion. He memorizes verses of Scripture. He becomes familiar, at least in general, with the doctrinal statements of his church. He learns to use theological terms and a religious vocabulary. But herein lies the danger! As he comes to Sunday school regularly, through the years, and learns and accepts the words which describe religious experiences, he tends to identify this with having had the experiences. That was precisely one of the problems Jesus encountered with the religion of the Pharisees. They verbalized about the great teachings of the prophets, but they had not learned the spirit of these teachings in their experience. How much this is happening in our Sunday schools today! Learning words which describe a religious experience is not the same as having the religious experience. Religion is a personal encounter between God and man; it is a relationship, an experience!

It is relatively easy to lead individuals to become familiar with the words which describe religious experiences. It is far more difficult to lead them into that encounter with God in which they will learn the spirit of religion in their experience. For this reason, the temptation is great for both teacher and learner to be content with the former. While the teacher must continue to use words as perhaps the primary means of teaching religion, he must constantly be aware of this danger and use every means at his disposal to overcome it.

The danger of leading the members to have only an emotional catharsis in the class session.—Many people have unconsciously developed the attitude that all that is necessary in Sunday school is to attend, sit, and listen. In the class session they discuss the ideals of Jesus and how wonderful they are; they discuss the sins of the world and how terrible they are. But all they do is talk about it. Not very often is any definite action taken.

This attitude develops slowly and imperceptibly over a period of years. Young children usually are quite ready to try to carry out the ideals suggested by the teacher. The adolescent is still idealistic and usually willing to "do something" for Christ. But even during this period, because so many of the class sessions just end in talk, he is beginning to develop the attitude that there is no need to get excited about the Sunday school discussion. Nothing will be done about it anyway. So he begins to sit back and just listen. When we reach adults we find that they have outgrown their childish enthusiasm and their adolescent idealism. They are more staid and dignified now. They rarely get excited about the evil in the world.

What is this process? Older adolescents and adults particularly come to Sunday school week after week, listen to the teacher tell how wonderful the ideals of Christ are and how evil the world is. They agree with what is taught. Their feelings or emotions are touched. They enjoy the lesson. After it, many in the class may go to the teacher, shake his hand, and say, "That was a wonderful lesson this morning. You surely did tell the truth." But when they leave, they do nothing about what was taught. They repeat the same thing the next Sunday, only to come back the third Sunday to listen, agree, enjoy, and have their emotions stirred again. Thus, the process goes, Sunday after Sunday.

Herein lies the danger! These people have their emotions stirred so often without making any overt response that they identify this emotional stirring with having had the religious experience they discussed in class. Whether they discuss the need for winning the lost to Christ, or the need for a vigorous worldwide missions program, or the need for eliminating gambling in the community, they receive a satisfying experience merely from talking about it.

This, however, is not a true and complete Christian experience. Emotions play an important and necessary part in religious experience but a true experience is not complete until it expresses itself in life and action. An emotional experience that does not lead to response; that is, an emotional experience that ends only in stirring one's feelings, is incomplete.

What makes this so unfortunate and even tragic in the lives of Christians is that, having come to Sunday school and church (this happens in the preaching service also) week after week and having their emotions stirred with no accompanying overt action, *they come both to desire and to be satisfied with having only their emotions stirred.*

This attitude is expressed colloquially in many different ways. Some say "I don't feel like I have been to church unless the preacher steps on my toes," or "I like a preacher (or teacher) who isn't afraid to hit you right where it hurts." The difficulty with this attitude is that the person still does not move even after he has been hit.

Teachers must be aware of this tendency on the part of the class members merely to come, sit, and listen. They must use every available means to keep it from happening. Sunday school teaching should not end in just "talk." To avoid this is not as simple and easy as the teacher might think. People are much more willing to have their emotions stirred as the class discusses some evil in the community than they are to go out and do something to change the evil condition. Nevertheless, Christian teaching is not complete until Christian action results.

WORKERS TOGETHER WITH GOD

Our problem, then, is to discover how to teach so that the great ideals of Jesus, presented in the classroom, will carry over into the lives of those who come to Sunday school. How can this be done? The first thing we need to learn is that we must teach in harmony with the way God intended for people to learn. Our God is an orderly God. Insofar as is possible, we must come to understand how God has made human personality so that we can co-operate with him in this great task of teaching. The Bible is the greatest textbook in the world. The saving, transforming message of Jesus is the greatest message the world has ever known. How, then, can we share this experience so that it will accomplish its divine purpose?

Does it make a difference as to how we teach the Bible? Because it is an inspired Book can we teach it in just any fashion and still have it accomplish its purpose? Are some ways of teaching the Bible better than other ways? There are those teachers who seem to feel that because they are teaching the Bible they do not have to know or follow proved educational principles. They do not want to be bothered with these "newfangled" ideas. Their attitude, simply stated, is, "I just teach the Bible and let the chips fall where they may." To support their view, they ask, "Does not God's Word say, 'My word shall not return unto me void'?" These teachers not only need to get the proper interpretation of that verse, but they also need to be reminded of the parable of the sower. In it Jesus is trying to help us understand that the type of soil upon which the Word of God is sown also determines the quantity and quality of fruit that will be borne.

The teacher usually has this viewpoint because he feels that such an attitude magnifies the Bible and emphasizes the power and work of God. Instead, it borders on presuming on God because it seeks to make God do what he is not supposed to do. Satan, following this same attitude, sought to persuade Jesus to presume on God by casting himself down from the pinnacle of the Temple. To do so would have been asking God to use his power in a way it was not supposed to be used. Such an attitude, in spite of the sincerity of those who hold it, places the responsibility for ineffective teaching and lack of results upon God, when in reality the responsibility must rest squarely upon the shoulders of the teacher.

Perhaps an illustration might help the teacher see more clearly the issues involved. A certain farmer goes forth to sow From early morning till midday he scatters his grains of corn on grassy pasture land. A friend, passing by, sees what he is doing. In amazement the friend asks, "What has happened to you? Don't you know you shouldn't be planting corn in a grassy field? You'll never get any corn that way." But the farmer replies, "Oh, yes I will. This is God's seed and God's good earth. He will take care of it." But the friend persists, "To do this is to presume upon God. You must plow and plant and fertilize and continue to cultivate." But the man again replies, "This is God's seed and God's earth. He will send sunshine and rain. I'm just planting the seed, and I'll leave the results to the Lord." But the friend concludes, "If you don't get any harvest it won't be the Lord's fault. The fault will be with you because you did not meet God's conditions for planting corn."

Of course, there is a vast difference between a grain of corn and the Bible. The above illustration is given merely to point out that the God who created the universe and the design by which corn grows also created man and the design by which he learns. It is the task of the Christian teacher to discover insofar as possible the way by which people learn and teach in harmony with that design.

The modern farmer has made and is making rapid progress. He studies about soil erosion, contour plowing, crop rotation, soil composition, and many other matters. He seeks to learn all he can about God's earth and how things grow. The result is that, today, two bales of cotton grow where formerly only one grew. Today, he gets two bushels of corn where formerly he got only one. What has he done? He has discovered how God works, and he is co-operating intelligently with God. As Christian teachers, we need to study and understand human personality. We need increasingly to discover how people learn—how God has ordained that people learn—in order that we as teachers might co-operate more intelligently with God. Only thus can we expect greater results from our efforts.

Someone may object to this viewpoint and say that this seems to minimize God. Rather, it magnifies God. Does the farmer's study and understanding of the earth make God unnecessary? Not at all. It is still God's seed. It is still God's earth. It is still his sun and rain. It is still he who germinates the seed and who gives the increase. The farmer just co-operates more intelligently with God and enables him to bring forth a greater fruitage.

The same is true in teaching the Bible. In trying to understand and follow the way that people learn, we do not make God unnecessary. We are still his creation. The Bible is still his Word. God alone can regenerate. It is God alone who gives the increase. But we as Christian teachers are trying to co-operate more intelligently with him. In the final analysis, it is God, the Holy Spirit, who is the great Teacher. It is the task of the human teacher to provide those conditions in which and through which the Holy Spirit can best do his divine work.

This type of teaching is not easy. It takes time to study and gain these insights. It often requires laborious effort to try to apply them. The farmer might say this type of farming is not easy. He does not enjoy the hard work of plowing. He would prefer to scatter the seed on grassy, unplowed ground. He may not want to spend his money to fertilize. He may not want to take the time to learn all of these new methods of farming. But when he plants his seed and has only a small fruitage, and the farm next to his, following the best in farming methods, has a large increase at harvest time, he sees how unwisely he has acted. Today's farmers are paying the price to discover how God causes corn to grow in order to co-operate intelligently with him. Certainly, as Christian teachers, we must be willing to pay the price to discover how God has ordained that we grow in Christlikeness. We must be willing to co-operate more intelligently with him.

The Centrality of the Conversion Experience

Throughout this book we will emphasize the matter of securing results in Christian living. Because of this emphasis, one might get the impression that we are interested only in results and that we have not given sufficient emphasis to the spiritual relationship with God in Christ, which is the only foundation for action that is thoroughly Christian. It is recognized also that some Sunday school teachers simply try to get their pupils to be "good" without leading them to understand that conduct that is truly Christian comes not from a desire to "please the teacher" or from any other similar extrinsic motivation, but only from God working and living in the individual.

Since it will not be possible to reiterate this emphasis at each point throughout the remainder of the book, we want to make explicit here what is implicit as the underlying philosophy in our approach to Christian teaching. *We believe that a conversion experience—a personal experience in which the individual accepts Jesus as Saviour and Lord—is the means by which an individual enters the Christian life and is the only adequate foundation and sufficient motivation for Christian growth.* By the term "conversion," we do not mean that a person has to have a dramatic or cataclysmic experience as the apostle Paul had on the road to Damascus. We mean an experience in which the individual meets God in Christ, in which he accepts Jesus as Saviour and surrenders to him as Lord. This is simply to say that man can never enter the kingdom of God either by virtue of his own goodness or by virtue of any process of religious education. As Shelton Smith has so aptly put it, "The Kingdom is God's, and human entrance into it is possible only through divine deliverance." [8]

What happens to the individual in the conversion experience?—Without going into a technical or theological answer to this question, there are at least five things that grow out of this experience that have significance for religious education.

First, the individual receives a new nature. The transforming and revolutionary aspect of the conversion experience has not been sufficiently emphasized in modern Christianity. This experience had tremendous implications in the mind of Jesus. In speaking with Nicodemus, he said it was so fundamentally life changing that it was like a man being born again. Indeed, it was a new birth!

The conversion experience is not a superficial or mechanical relationship. It is not merely a perfunctory acceptance of a religious formula. Paul said, "Therefore if any man be in Christ, he is a new creature; old things are passed away; behold, all things are become new" (2 Cor. 5:17). This does not mean that the individual must have a highly emotional experience. It simply means that when an individual gets a *new* nature something ought to happen in his life. The center of life is changed from self to God. New desires, hopes, and ideals are born within him. He no longer can say "I'll do as I please." Rather he must say "I'll do as God teaches." And he says this not primarily on the basis of an obligation which has

[8] Smith, H. Shelton, *Faith and Nurture* (New York: Charles Scribner's Sons, 1946) p 125. Used by permission.

been imposed on him, but on the basis of a new relationship and new love that has been born within him. This is what he wants most to do. On the basis of this new life, to do the will of God and not of man becomes the deepest desire of his heart.

This suggests a second thing the individual should get in the conversion experience: a desire to know the teachings of the Bible and their implication for the Christian way of life. The individual enters the kingdom of God as a "babe in Christ." In spite of previous religious training, he does not know what the application of the teachings of Jesus means in all the various relationships of his life.

Through the conversion experience the individual has entered a new *way* of life. The person for whom this experience has been deep and genuine should be anxious to study the Scriptures, alone and in groups of like-minded Christians, to find out what is involved in this new way of life.

This desire to know, as worthy as it is, does not go far enough. This brings us to a third point. There must also be a willingness to follow the teachings of the Bible, a willingness to follow the Christian way of life when it is learned, wherever it may lead. This is not as simple as it might seem at first glance. It would be relatively easy to live the Christian life today, if the only thing that is meant by "Christian life" is living according to the accepted social standards and attending church. Unfortunately, this concept is far more prevalent among church members than we would like to admit. But if the Christian life means applying the ideals of Jesus in such a way that they would lead an individual to go beyond the accepted social standards in many relationships and lead him to go contrary to accepted social standards in other relationships, then living the Christian life becomes one of the most daring and certainly one of the most difficult tasks in which an individual can engage.

Yet, in spite of the difficulty, if there does not grow out of the conversion experience a deep basic commitment of one's life to follow the teachings of Jesus wherever they might lead, then it would be well for the individual to re-examine his experience. It has been stated that, basically, the conversion experience involves a commitment to a new way of life. If there is no compelling desire both to know and to follow this new way, there is reason to question the genuineness of the experience. This is important because, as will be pointed out in a later chapter, this affects the individual's attitude toward the study of the Bible and his attitude toward following that which is discovered through such study.

In the fourth place, in and through the conversion experience there is released a power beyond his own which, if utilized, enables the individual to have the strength to follow more closely the exacting demands of the Christian life. Many of the demands of the Christian life go contrary to one's natural desires and human passions. It is not normal or natural for one to "love his enemies," to "do good to those who persecute him," "to forgive those who say all manner of evil against him falsely." To retaliate is human. Power from on high is needed if the individual is even to approximate the Christian ideal in these and other areas.

Finally, in the conversion experience, we find the only adequate foundation and motivation for Christian living. In the time of Jesus the Pharisees followed the letter of the Law, but the Spirit of God was far from them. Today it is possible for individuals to follow certain of the teachings of Jesus without having an adequate spiritual motivation.

It is always a temptation for those who teach religion (and for those who preach, for that matter) to be satisfied with securing certain types of overt responses that carry with them the connotation "Christian." It is so much easier to lead people to practice the external forms of religion or even to make certain responses that might be termed "Christian" than it is to lead them into those continuing encounters with God in Christ that will cause them to respond, "Not my will, but thine be done." The Christian standard for life is high; its demands are difficult, often coming into conflict with all the human passions of our being. In these situations—as in all situations that call for decision—the individual's life must be grounded in a firm and genuine relationship with God in Christ. In seeking any kind of conduct response, it is an important part of the teacher's task to seek to insure that the decisions for action that are made by the members are made on the basis of a spiritual motivation.

Does the conversion experience automatically produce Christian character?—Having had this experience, does the individual automatically become Christian in his family relations, in his recreational relations, in his social relations, in his business relations? The answer is no. He will become more Christian in certain relationships and activities, but he does not automatically become Christian in all.

The attitude held by some that if a person is "really saved," he will know what is right and will do it is simply not true. He will know some things that are right, but he will not know everything. One does not come to have divine wisdom in the conversion experience. Just so in the practice of religion, the individual does not automatically "do what's right" because he has been "saved."

Peter did not have his attitude toward the Gentiles transformed at the time of his conversion. God had to teach him this spiritual truth later in his Christian development. Investigations and observations indicate that, following the conversion experience, changes take place in a person's life only in those areas in which there is conviction of sin. And even this change does not take place automatically. This conviction must be sufficiently deep to call for the change.

Take, for example, a man who is a drunkard and who has a transforming, regenerating experience with Christ. If, in this experience, he is deeply convicted of the sinfulness of drinking, he will give up this evil habit. However, this experience may have no effect on his business dealings. He may continue to extract excessive rent from the run-down houses he owns in the city's slum area. He may see no relation between this situation and his newly-accepted religion. Therefore, since he has no conviction of sin in this area, no change will take place in it.

Or, here is another man who, in his experience with Jesus, is convicted of the sin of immorality in his life. Undoubtedly he will cease his immoral living, but he may fail to be honest with God in the matter of stewardship. Therefore, in the conversion experience, it seems that change in an individual's life takes place in those areas in which there is conviction of sin.

One of the tasks of religious education is to lift the other areas of an individual's life where he is not now living according to the ideals of Jesus to the level of awareness of these shortcomings. In the Sunday school he brings his normal everyday experiences to be placed under the searchlight of the teachings of the Bible. As he considers those experiences and seeks the Christian course of action, the Holy Spirit has a chance to convict of sin and lead to change.

THE PROBLEM TEACHERS FACE

The primary problem, then, that the teacher faces is not so much how to teach the Bible as it is how to lead individuals —children and adults alike—in those experiences through which they will come to know Jesus as Saviour and through which they will increasingly grow in his likeness. In short, the task of the teacher is to discover and use the most effective means for securing behavior response that is in harmony with the ideals of Jesus.

In Christian teaching, we are increasingly emphasizing that the religiously educated man is much more than one who "knows." He is one whose attitudes and systems of value are consistent with the Christian ethic and who, at all times, seeks to translate these attitudes into right conduct.

There is no "royal road to learning." Improvement in the art of teaching and in securing results is a slow and sometimes tedious process. The principles suggested in this book may help the teacher improve his teaching, but principles do not apply themselves. If the teacher is daring enough to try to use some of these suggestions he may find them, at least at first, exceedingly difficult to apply. It is not easy to work out a plan to secure purposeful Bible study or to devise a life situation to make the lesson personal. If the teacher has difficulty, he should not become discouraged. With patient practice these principles can become an integral part of his lesson planning. After all, it is results we are seeking—not an easy way!

III

UNDERSTANDING THE
TEACHING-LEARNING PROCESS

hat is teaching? When do teachers teach? Millions
of dollars have been spent on churches and religious education buildings; rooms have been beau-
tified; equipment has been purchased. Large amounts of
money are spent purchasing educational literature, quarter-
lies, and lesson helps. Thousands of hours are spent each week
in study and lesson preparation. Thousands of volunteer,
earnest, consecrated Christians meet their classes weekly for
the avowed purpose of teaching! Do they—do we—understand what teaching is?

TWO APPROACHES [1]

There are at least two approaches to the problem of teaching that the teacher should understand. It is always danger-
ous to "label" a point of view but perhaps it will not be unfair
to say that one approach is in line with the more traditional,
transmissive concept of teaching, while the other follows the
newer insights of educational psychology. The teacher should
study both points of view carefully to determine which, if
either, will more nearly achieve his spiritual objectives.

Character development.—Approach No. 1 seems to hold
that character is developed primarily by teaching the pupil
Bible knowledge. The assumption is that one will develop
Christian character if he knows what the Bible teaches.

[1] Adapted from Lindhorst, F. A., *The Minister Teaches Religion* (New
York: Abingdon-Cokesbury Press, 1945), pp. 15–19. Used by permission.

29

Approach No. 2 holds that Christian character is developed by leading the individual to make choices and to engage in experiences that are Christian. It holds that while Bible knowledge is basic, it does not necessarily result in Christian living.

The teacher.—One approach holds that the teacher is the source of wisdom. This is one reason why the teacher does all the talking. The teacher has studied the lesson and has learned certain things. He feels that it is his task to tell the class members what he has learned. This approach holds that "telling" is "teaching." This view also implies that the pupil should keep quiet and listen to what the teacher has prepared. Usually the teacher resents any interruption on the part of the pupils. The teacher feels: "I must cover the material in this lesson."

In the other approach, the teacher is a guide. The teacher has studied and knows certain things, but also the class members are recognized as knowing certain things. Learning takes place through a sharing of ideas and experiences between teacher and class members. The teacher is the more mature guide of the group and thus leads the group as they seek to discover for themselves the Christian attitude or the Christian course of action in a given situation. In this approach the teacher learns as well as do the pupils.

The pupil.—The first approach holds that since the pupil is immature his experiences and his knowledge are of little value. Therefore, the main responsibility of the pupil is to sit quietly and listen to what the teacher has to say. His responsibility is to remember what the teacher teaches. The view of the teacher toward the pupil in this approach is, "You sit still while I instill." The teacher views his task as being that of filling the emptiness of the pupil.

In the other view, the pupil is considered as being a person in his own right. His experience and his knowledge have value. The pupil is a responsible member of the learning group, both having something to contribute and having something to learn. The needs and interests of the pupil serve as a guide for the teacher in knowing what to teach and how to teach. In this view the pupil does not necessarily sit quietly and listen to what the teacher has to say, but rather both teacher and pupil are actively engaged in seeking to discover the truth that needs to be discovered. Learning for the pupil is self-learning. The truth that is learned is not imposed from without, but is rather discovered by the pupil under the leadership and guidance of the teacher.

Interest.—In one view, the interest of the group is secured primarily by promised rewards or in some cases prizes. When discipline problems arise, the teacher may sometimes resort to threatened punishment. Interest, in this approach, is important only to the extent that it leads the pupils to sit quietly and listen to what the teacher has to say.

In the second approach, interest inheres in the learning activity itself. That is, the teacher undertakes to teach those things for which the pupils have a felt need and in which they are genuinely interested. The teacher knows the pupils so intimately that he knows how to relate that which is being taught to the problems and needs his class members are facing in their everyday lives. Therefore, when the class members realize that they are getting help for problems which are plaguing them in their present experience, they immediately become interested in trying to find the answers to their problems. Likewise, the teacher knows the class members so intimately and knows their interests in such a way that he is able to relate the things which are being studied to their normal interests. Thus, interest inheres in the learning activity itself.

The lesson.—In one approach, the teacher conceives "the lesson" to be that which is printed in the quarterly. Thus, he feels that in order to teach the lesson he has to teach that which is presented in the quarterly. The teacher also relies upon other lesson helps that are provided and feels that he must try to cover the things that are suggested in them. He feels that when he has covered this material he has taught "the lesson."

In the other approach, "the lesson" is the aim or objective that the teacher has in mind for a given class period. The purpose of the teacher is to accomplish his aim and not necessarily to cover a given body of material. In order to reach this objective, the teacher will use the material that is suggested in the quarterly and also those materials that are suggested in the other lesson helps. But he will use only that material which will contribute to the achieving of his lesson aim. All else will have to be omitted. These teachers use the lesson helps simply as guides as denominational leaders intend for them to be used. In this view, the lesson has been taught only when the aim or objective has been accomplished in the lives of the class members, not when the material has been covered.

Physical arrangement.—In one approach, the physical arrangement is likely to be the traditional one with the teacher standing at the front of the class and the members sitting in rows facing the teacher. This arrangement contributes to letting the teacher do the talking and having the class members to keep quiet. It accentuates the dominance of the teacher and the inferior position held by the class members.

In the other approach, the seating arrangement is more likely to be in a circle where the teacher takes his place along with all of the other class members. In this way, each class member faces every other class member and feels himself as a responsible part of the group. Here, the arrangement contributes to the attitude that the class members have a right to express their opinion and speak up at any time they desire. It helps to get away from the attitude of the teacher-dominated class and contributes to the development of a spirit of democracy in the teaching situation.

STEPS IN THE TEACHING-LEARNING PROCESS

Every teacher desires to teach in such a way that what is taught will make a difference in the lives of the class members. How can this be done? What are some of the factors that make for good teaching? Dr. Ernest M. Ligon suggests five steps that are involved in the teaching-learning process.[2]

Exposure.—Obviously, a person must be exposed to a Bible truth before he can learn it. This suggests a responsibility for the teacher that is not usually emphasized in a book dealing with principles of teaching. It is the responsibility for reaching people—both absentees and prospects—for Bible study. A church may have the very finest and most capable group of teachers that can be had, but their teaching will not help those who are not present on Sunday morning. Someone has said, "You can't teach an absentee." Neither will this teaching be of any value to the vast host of children, young people, and adults who have never been reached. Just to reach numbers for numbers' sake is a tragedy. But whether we like it or not, we must reach people before we can teach them. Therefore, the first essential in good teaching is to enlist every member and prospect for Bible study.

However, it must be recognized that exposure is simply the first step in the learning process. The difficulty in the past has been that too often the teacher has been content with simply exposing his class members to knowledge without following through with the other steps in the learning process. Some teachers have felt that if they could tell their members what was in the lesson or in the Bible the members would automatically learn.

This assumption is not as valid as teachers may have thought. For example, suppose a great preacher or teacher were invited to give a series of lectures, say on the Gospel of Mark, one chapter each week for sixteen weeks. "We attend every time. But we make no preparation, no recitation, take no notes, have no review, and no examination. How much would we learn of permanent value? Of course, there are individual differences, but for most of us, within a few months

[2] Ligon, Ernest M., *A Greater Generation* (New York: The Macmillan Company, 1948), pp. 10–14. Used by permission.

it would be almost as if we had never heard the lectures. We would have had some fine inspiration, acquired a deep admiration for the teacher, and a profound respect for Mark and his subject. But of usable, permanent knowledge we would have gained almost none." [3] Thus, while exposure is necessary, if the teacher is going to secure meaningful and lasting learning on the part of his members, he must do more than simply expose them to the knowledge. What are some of the other steps the teacher must consider?

Repetition.—Public schools have long recognized the necessity for repetition in effective learning. Parents recognize the same necessity in child training. A child does not learn to practice good manners because his mother tells him one time to do so. How many times parents must remind the child to say "thank you" before it becomes a part of his normal conduct! A child does not learn unselfish attitudes because he has been told about them once by his parents. It is likewise true that the developing of Christian attitudes and Christian habits is the result of constant, persistent repetition.

In Sunday school teaching there are two practical and difficult problems that inhere in the nature of Sunday school work as it is carried on today. First, teaching is done at intervals of one week. It is quite easy for people to forget during the week what was learned the previous Sunday. A second problem is that those who use the Uniform Lesson Series have a different lesson for each Sunday. The teacher might well ask, "How can we use repetition in our teaching in light of the fact that we teach only once a week and have a different lesson each Sunday?"

The seriousness of these difficulties must not be minimized. However, they are not insuperable. With regard to the first problem the following suggestion is given: If the teacher has had a knowledge aim for the lesson he could easily have assignments for the class to work on during the week. This practice could be followed with all age groups. Our people need

[3] *Ibid.*, p. 11

to develop the attitude that serious daily Bible study is a normal and accepted part of their everyday experiences. It could well be that such study during the week would greatly enrich the study on Sunday. The teacher may ask, "How can I get them to do this extra study? I can't even get them to study their lesson." This means we have not captured our members for the thrilling adventure of Bible study. It means that what we have been saying in this book is all too true. Our members are content to come to Sunday school, sit and listen—and do nothing. It means that teaching must be much more effective in challenging and directing the interests of Christians toward effective Bible study.

But how to get members to study special assignments during the week? *Expect it!* Often we get not because we expect not. The class members must come to understand that the teacher means business. Of course, the assignments must be in line with the age level and the abilities of the members. The members must also be provided with the means for study or with aids in study. People often fail to study the Bible because they do not understand what they study. Books should be available in the church library. They should be led to purchase inexpensive commentaries to guide them in their study. The teacher should also have reports in class on these assignments. The class will not be transformed overnight, but the teacher can get some highly desirable results if over a period of weeks, and even months, he will patiently yet persistently lead his class to know that he expects study on outside assignments during the week. In this way the problem of forgetting between Sundays will be greatly diminished.

If the teacher has a conduct response aim in mind, the carry-over, if achieved by the teacher, will lead the members to practice the spiritual truth during the week. Thus, again, the problem is largely solved.

The problem of having a different lesson to teach still does not rule out the possibility of the teacher using repetition in his teaching. There are three things that should be said. First,

the teacher should learn to use "unit aims." If there are two
or more lessons which emphasize the same spiritual truth, the
teacher may have one aim for all of these lessons. Then, as
each of the lessons is taught, the teacher will be repeating
from a different point of view the same spiritual truth that
he desires the class members to learn. Secondly, the teacher
should make it a practice to review the lesson for the past
Sunday each time he meets with his class. In this way, each
lesson will be related to the previous lesson. Finally, those
who are responsible for preparing the curricula materials
have designed them in such a way that the great biblical doctrines and spiritual ideals are repeated year after year at different stages of the individual's development. Thus, there is
opportunity for repetition.

Understanding.—Understanding is one of the most important steps in the learning process. Yet in the realm of religious teaching it, perhaps, is one of the most neglected.
Many of us learn what the Bible says about various things,
but we do not understand what these teachings mean so far
as our daily, personal lives are concerned. Sometime ago, one
of our national leaders said that all of our national and international problems would be solved if everyone would practice the Golden Rule. The statement was received with great
acclaim, and, certainly, all of us would agree with it. But what
would it mean in your personal life if you were to start practicing the Golden Rule? What change would it make in your
relationships with your neighbors? What would you start doing for the underprivileged group who lives in your area?
How would you practice the Golden Rule in your attitude toward the Russians? You see, understanding what the Golden
Rule would mean in specific action for our personal lives is,
indeed, difficult.

We believe that the Beatitudes present to us an outline for
the highest type of Christian life. We believe: "Blessed are
the poor in spirit; for theirs is the kingdom of heaven"
(Matt. 5:3). But what does this teaching mean for your per-

sonal life? What would you start doing next week that you have not been doing if you were to carry out this teaching of Jesus? I dare say that it would be difficult for you to think of anything. It is important for us to believe these great ideals and teachings of Jesus. But they are of little value to us unless we understand what they mean in terms of specific attitudes and actions for our daily personal lives. As has been indicated, one of the weaknesses of much of present Sunday school teaching is that we teach in vague generalities without leading our people to understand specifically what these teachings of Jesus would mean in terms of daily activities.

Conviction.—Understanding is not enough. Conviction must also be present. One must believe the teaching to the point where he is willing to follow the teaching regardless of the difficulty involved. He must have a conviction that is so strong it will lead to action. For example, an adolescent may understand that if he followed the ideal of love in his family relations, he would keep his room straight and hang up his clothes. But he does not have a conviction of this teaching that is deep enough to make him do it.

There are many spiritual truths we say we believe, but our convictions are not sufficiently deep to lead us to make our lives conform to these ideals. So far as the Christian way of life is concerned we believe that Jesus was right when he said, "If any man will come after me, let him deny himself, and take up his cross and follow me" (Matt. 16:24). Yet in spite of our professed belief in this teaching, our lives indicate that we really believe that self-interest is superior to self-sacrifice. Again Jesus says, "Blessed are ye, when men shall revile you, and persecute you, and shall say all manner of evil against you falsely, for my sake. Rejoice, and be exceeding glad; for great is your reward in heaven" (Matt. 5:11–12). We may believe that, but we do not believe it with such conviction that we as Christians are willing so to fight sin with all of the fury at our command, in such a way that those who are engaging in evil business and evil activities will

fight us, revile us, and persecute us. We do not believe that
this is the way to be happy. Again Jesus says, "Bless them that
curse you, do good to them that hate you, and pray for them
which despitefully use you, and persecute you" (Matt. 6:44).
We believe that this is the right way to live, the way for a
man to be happy. Yet we do not believe it with the conviction necessary for this principle to control our daily lives.

In trying to teach for Christian living, in seeking results in
the lives of those we teach, conviction is a central and necessary factor. It is quite evident that it is possible for Christians to believe religious doctrines and spiritual ideals and
yet not have a conviction that is sufficiently deep to lead
them to follow these truths in their daily experience. Thus
the teacher is made increasingly aware of the difficulty of his
task. It is not sufficient for him to expose the class to Christian ideals by telling them what the Bible says; it is not sufficient for him to keep repeating these truths Sunday after
Sunday; it is not even sufficient for him to lead them to understand what these spiritual truths mean for their personal
lives. He must do all of these plus leading the group to accept and believe those spiritual ideals with a conviction that
is so deep that these ideals will become active and directive
forces in changing each individual's life in harmony with
them.

Application.—By "application" we do not mean the usual
application that is made at the close of a Sunday school lesson. Moralizing, bringing out truths, making general applications, and exhorting are not sufficient to get carry-over into
the lives of our class members. The teacher must plan with
the members those opportunities in which they will be able
to express in action the truth that was studied. For example,
if the lesson is on "Helping those in need," what is the class
going to do about it? Is there an underprivileged family in
the community that the class could help? Is there a minority
group who needs assistance? Shall the class go to the county
jail and put on a religious program? In other words, will the

class members just talk about those in need or will they do something about helping them? Planning for this expression of the Christian ideal is just as much a part of teaching as any other phase of the lesson. In fact, this is the climax and key of all good teaching.

Sunday school teachers must face the inescapable fact that their members have not learned the teachings of Jesus until these teachings actually are put into practice in their daily experiences. Teachers have not taught until their class members have begun to live. Ligon gives an illustration of this type of teaching and learning:

> The boy had a Saturday morning job of taking the week's accumulation of papers from the cellar and burning them. One morning a neighbor boy kicked them all down as fast as he could pile them up. The father says that his own succinct recommendation to his son was, "Sock him!" His son's astounding reply was, "Dad, I don't think that is the way to do it." Knowing from the frequent battles between the boys that this was not motivated by fear, the father decided to find out what was the way to do it. His son finally solved the problem this way. He remembered that the other boy also had a Saturday morning job. He said to him, "If you'll help me do my job, I'll help you do your job." The father finished his report by saying, "I've gone to church all my life, but for practical religion, I'll have to take off my hat to my son." [4]

This is the kind of learning that we seek. This is Christianity in action. This also is the answer to our question: What is teaching?

A Problem

At each stage of life, learning goes on normally and naturally. The baby learns to eat with a spoon; the small boy learns to tie his shoes. The young boy learns to skate and to play baseball; the young girl learns to bake a cake. The older boy or girl learns to drive a car; the adult learns a vocation,

[4] *Ibid.*, p. 15.

and so on through life learning takes place naturally in the normal everyday experiences of life.

But this type of learning, while effective, is often haphazard, inadequate, and sometimes inaccurate. To offset these shortcomings society has established public schools, and churches have established Sunday schools. In these schools, in order to avoid depending on haphazard or chance learning experiences and to avoid unpleasant or undesirable learning experiences, we introduce the element of control in the experience of the learner to direct his learning activities. Thus, we have a classroom situation with books to be studied, with a curriculum to be followed, and with stated objectives to be sought.

It is just at this point that we begin to have our problem with helping another to learn. When we take learning out of the normal experiences of living and place it in the unnatural environment of a classroom, we often make learning unnatural also. For in the classroom we go about the task of teaching and learning in an altogether different way than we would in ordinary life experience. We substitute authority for freedom; we substitute discipline for interest; we substitute the giving of assignments for meeting needs; we substitute the studying of lessons for studying life; and finally we substitute things to be learned for living itself.

Yet, we must place learning in the classroom, for we cannot depend entirely upon the haphazard experiences of life for the complete religious education of children or adults. Therefore the teacher must seek to bridge the gap for the learner between the unnatural classroom situation and the normal experiences of life. The teacher must seek to identify those principles which operate when people learn in the normal experiences of life and seek to utilize them in the classroom. What are some of these principles?

There are, of course, many types of learning. There is a theory of learning for each type. In discussing how people learn we have to ask, "What kind of learning do we mean?"

In this discussion, we have in mind that learning which results in changed attitudes and conduct.

SOME MISCONCEPTIONS

Before we note some of the more positive principles there are certain misconceptions as to what learning is that should be mentioned. First, just as telling is not necessarily teaching, so listening is not necessarily learning. There is a great deal of listening that goes on in our Sunday schools as the lessons are being taught, but the teacher would be embarrassed if, at the end of the quarter, a simple test were given to find out how little learning actually took place. Listening is an aspect of learning. But it is certainly a mistake for the teacher to assume that, because he is talking and the members are listening, learning is taking place.

In the second place, reciting is not necessarily learning. Often the teacher feels that the class member has learned if he is able to answer correctly the teacher's questions. However, such reciting does not necessarily mean that the member will use in his life experience the thing that he has recited. Sunday school members at a very early age learn what the teacher expects them to say, and very dutifully they answer the questions as the teacher wants them answered. In too many instances they do not tell what they are really thinking. Sometimes they recite answers which they do not even understand. A psychology professor recently told of asking a student to give a definition of a certain psychological term. The student gave the definition perfectly. Then the professor asked the student to explain what the definition meant. The student replied, "Professor, I don't have the slightest idea." [5] While it is true that asking and answering questions are helpful, mere reciting does not necessarily mean learning.

In the third place, memorizing does not necessarily mean learning. The learning of Bible verses is important for the life of every individual. However, the point being made here

[5] *Ibid.*, p. 12.

is that the Bible verses that are learned must become directing and controlling influences in the life and experience of the individual. The teacher may be exceedingly proud of little Johnny when he can quote in class, "Be ye kind one to another." But if, after Sunday school, Johnny goes out in front of the church and pulls his sister's hair until she cries, then that verse of Scripture has not become a controlling and directing influence in little Johnny's life. While memorizing Scripture is helpful, the teacher must recognize that merely memorizing is not enough. The Scripture that is learned must be learned in relationship to the present ongoing experience of the individual.

Principles of Learning

Learning must start where the pupil is.—This principle may seem very trite, yet it is often violated. A learned scholar may give an exceedingly interesting and brilliant lecture on atomic energy. He may explain about the workings of electrons and neutrons. But if he does, I will be sitting there restless and uninterested because I do not know anything about such matters. If he wants to reach me, if he wants to help me, he must start on a much lower level of explanation. The things I need to know may seem very elementary to the learned scholar, but if he wants to carry me with him on this intellectual journey, he must start where I am.

Just so, in teaching in Sunday school many a class member is left behind as the teacher progresses on a spiritual journey because the teacher did not start where the pupil was. If the aim of the teacher is to teach Bible knowledge, he must know what knowledge his members already have and what they do not have. If the teacher's aim is to lead the class to understand the Christian concept of prayer, he must know what their present attitude toward prayer is. He must know what problems they face in having faith in the power of prayer as well as the problems they are having in the practice of prayer. The teacher cannot teach a general lesson on prayer and assume it will do his members "good." It certainly will not do them the good it would have if he had known their particular problems so that he could have started where they were.

Teachers often take too much for granted. They assume that those whom they teach know and understand far more about the Bible and the Christian life than they actually do. This is true both of children and adults. Probably the only difference between children and adults at this point is that adults have learned to sit quietly while they are disinterested; children have not. They both fail to learn when the teacher does not approach them on the level of their understanding and in light of their past experiences.

The things the members need to know and the experiences they need to have may seem elementary to the teacher who has studied and understood these matters for a long time, but the lesson will be meaningless unless the teacher begins where the members are. We are now ready to state our first principle: *The teacher must know the members of his class intimately enough to know their level of understanding and their present attitudes in the area being studied and he must teach them in light of and in terms of their present understanding and development.*

Learning is based on interest.—In normal life experiences we learn best that in which we are interested. Which would a six-year-old boy learn best: to ride a bicycle or to wash dishes? Certainly, he would learn to ride a bicycle. Why? He is more interested in this activity. When we analyze this rather simple illustration more closely, the factor of interest becomes even more significant. In spite of the groans that accompany the chores of dishwashing, learning to ride a bicycle is far more difficult than learning to wash dishes. It demands much more physical exertion. It involves a great deal more physical pain. More than likely, it will involve many falls and skinned knees and elbows. But after each fall the boy, still undaunted, gets up and tries it again. Why?

His interest in riding a bicycle and his desire to master it make him willing to pay whatever price is necessary to achieve success. This indicates that boys and girls as well as men and women are not afraid of difficult tasks or of hard work *if* their interest in a given activity or study is sufficiently strong to make the work worth-while.

What does this say to those who try to teach Sunday school? If this is the way God has made us, if this is the way we learn, then we must recognize and observe this principle in our teaching. It means for the teacher that the question "How can I arouse the interest of my class in this study?" is just as important as the question "What am I going to teach them in this study?" Unfortunately, many of our teachers have been concerned only with the second question. They have spent long hours in study preparing what to teach, but they have given little or no consideration to the task of arousing the curiosity and stimulating the interest of the group in that particular study. Of course, what we teach is basic and fundamental. We must teach them the truth of God's Word. But so many times the difficulty is that we merely expose people to the Bible truth, and the exposure does not take. Whether our class members will actually *learn* what we teach is partially determined by the amount of interest they have in the study.

Someone may object and say, "These people ought to be interested in what we are teaching. We are teaching the Bible, God's eternal truth." Certainly, we will all agree that people ought to be interested in studying the Bible. But to talk about what people ought to do and what they ought to be will not solve our problem. We must take people as they are. If this then is the way people are, the teacher will ignore the principle of interest to the detriment of both himself and his class members.

A further word should be added. The teacher must recognize that there is a difference between the teacher's interest and the members' interest. The teacher may be intensely interested in the subject being studied, but the members may sit passively and learn nothing. The teacher must not assume that because he is interested, the class members will likewise be interested.

We are now ready to state our next principle: *Since learning is based upon interest, the teacher, in preparing his lesson, must make careful plans for arousing the curiosity and stimulating the interest of the class at the beginning of the lesson, realizing that there is little need for him to continue with it until such interest has been secured.*

Learning is based on need.—Closely related to interest is the matter of felt need. Again, if we observe people in their normal everyday relationships we will find that they learn that for which they have a need. Let us imagine that a husband and his wife have just brought a newborn baby from the hospital, and the wife is confined to her bed. No one else is there to assist. Which will the husband learn more readily, to fix the baby's formula or to conjugate a verb? Of course, he will learn to fix the baby's formula. Why? Because he has a sense of need.

Therefore, the teacher must know the members of his class so well and so intimately that he will be able to approach the lesson in such a way that it will meet the needs and solve the problems which the members are facing. The teacher may say, "That is not easy to do." Of course, it is not. Teaching is not easy. Nevertheless, this principle must be followed if effective learning is to take place. In the preparation of the lesson the teacher must ask himself the question, "What need or needs do my members have that are met by this lesson? How can I arrange the discussion and consideration of these materials in such a way that these needs will be met?"

If the teacher is presenting a passage from the book of Amos to a group of children or adults, he must find in the passage that which the members need in their lives today. They are not particularly interested in what Amos said or did over 2,500 years ago. Because they live in today's world, they inevitably have certain questions that need answering, certain problems that need solving, certain attitudes that need changing. However, when the teacher studies Amos more carefully and observes the lives of his members more closely, he will find that the questions Amos sought to answer, the attitudes he sought to change, and the problems he sought to solve are strangely similar to those people face today.

The teacher must identify the needs of his members, start with their needs, and let Amos help him meet those needs. He will find not only that the class session will become more alive, but also that the Bible will become more alive for his members. This is the way the Bible should be used: not simply as a source for passages from which devotional talks are made, but as God's guide for life, helping to answer our questions, to solve our problems, and to serve as the backdrop against which our attitudes are to be analyzed, evaluated, and changed when they do not conform to God's teachings.

Since the primary task of a teacher is not to present material, but rather to meet the needs of the members, our third principle may be stated as follows: *In preparing the lesson, the teacher should identify specifically the needs of the class members which may be met by that particular lesson. The materials should then be arranged and the lesson taught in such a way that those needs will be met.*

Learning takes place through activity.—We also learn through guided, purposeful activity. One educator has defined teaching as leading the class members to engage in desirable, purposeful activities. We all have heard of the boredom that students sometimes experience in school, listening to a dry professor deliver a still drier lecture. Some wit has said that a college lecture is that process by which the notes of the professor get to the notebook of the student without going through the mind of either. However, let us picture a student listening to a professor's lecture. He is taking notes. Is he learning? If not, why not? If so, why? If he is learning, what must be present? The answer is: activity or response on the part of the student must be present. It may be unfortunate but nevertheless true that it is entirely possible for one to listen to a lecture in school or in Sunday school without learning anything.

Someone may immediately raise the question, "What do you mean by 'activity'? Do you mean that my adult class will have to get up and act out the parable of the good Samaritan before they will learn?" Of course not. This activity or response may be mental, emotional, or physical. The teacher may stimulate the class to think. Questions may pass back and forth between the teacher and the members. Often, it will be the members who will ask the questions. There may be discussion among the members themselves. This mental activity may lead to learning. There may also be emotional response in which the feelings of the individual are touched and his ideals are heightened, his convictions deepened, or his attitude changed. It still remains that when the teacher acts, the member must react for learning to take place.

Smaller children use physical activity as a part of the learning process. The "interest center" approach to teaching is largely based on the principle of learning through guided, purposeful activity. Teachers seek to lead these children to develop the attitude of helpfulness by leading them to act out the story of the four friends who brought the sick man to Jesus. Children may develop the habit of expressing thanks at meals by participating in this experience in the housekeeping center. They may learn co-operation and sharing in the block center. In the nature center, as they become aware of God's beautiful world, they may be led in a real experience of worship. The key words here are *guided, purposeful* activity. Mere busy activity or aimless play is not sufficient.

When we teach older children and adults, we are confronted with a problem. As we look at the way people learn in their normal everyday relationships, we become aware that older children and adults also learn through physical activity. The youth learns to make and operate a radio. The adult learns how to make an effective visit to a prospective client. We call this learning through experience. Is this avenue of learning closed to us in our Sunday school teaching? Certainly not. We need to become more keenly aware that activity is not limited to the classroom on Sunday.

Far more often than we are now doing, we need to lead our members in purposeful projects which will find their expression outside the classroom. Indeed, the teacher will find that in carrying out these projects the members of the class often will learn more practical religion for their personal lives and develop more Christian attitudes than they ever could simply by listening to a teacher—any teacher—in a class session. If the teacher desires for his class to develop a real missionary spirit, he might lead them to engage in some missionary project in the community. If the teacher would have the class develop a concern for the needy and underprivileged, he might lead them in a project in which they render help for those who are in need. However, for this to be of maximum benefit each individual must participate in the project in person, not just give money. We miss something very real in our Christian lives when we simply give money and let others have the personal experience of helping those in need. Does the teacher desire to arouse within the group a deep concern because of sin in the community? Lead the class in a project to eliminate some flagrant sin in the community—not just talk about it in class. Surely it demands time; it demands work; and the class members may get their collective hands dirty in the process. But this is the way we can develop the spirit of Jesus and follow his example. Would the teacher have the class develop a consciousness of the social ills in the community? Let him lead the group then to correct one of these social ills. It will be difficult. Undoubtedly they will be criticized, but so was Jesus. We cannot learn Christianity just through talk. We learn through experience. In Sunday school we have a lot of talk; what we need is more action.

This is the way Jesus taught. After a period of instruction

he sent out the twelve and then the seventy that they might both render service and also learn through experience the joy of service. They came back thrilled with their experience. We can do no better than follow the example of Jesus in this way of teaching. To do less is to fail by that much.

Our fourth principle may be stated thus: *The teacher, in preparing the lesson, must make plans to stimulate purposeful activity on the part of the class members. This activity may be mental, emotional, or physical. It may take place both in and outside the class session. We learn best through experience; therefore, whenever possible lead the class in desirable Christian experiences.*

We learn through identification.—The fact that we learn through identification is a matter that has not been sufficiently appreciated or emphasized by educators in the past. Seemingly, they have been so concerned with educational techniques and psychological manipulations that they have failed to recognize the importance of the life and personality of the teacher in the teaching-learning process. This topic is so important that a later chapter will be given to its consideration.[6] It will be dealt with only briefly here.

Dr. Ross Snyder, professor at the University of Chicago Divinity School, once said that if you want to find out what kind of person one is, ask what kind of parents and other people he associated with in his earliest formative years. This is simply another way of saying that one learns the basic issues of life through personal identification.

One gets many of his ideals, his likes and dislikes, his concept of right and wrong, his attitude toward minority groups, and many other basic concepts from the person or persons with whom he identifies himself. This is of particular significance for the Christian teacher for he is concerned with helping the individual develop those fundamental attitudes which direct and control his life.

Therefore it might be said that in the final analysis the

[6] Chapter XV.

Sunday school is only as good as the teachers it has for personal identification. This makes the task of teaching both more easy and more difficult. It makes it easier because it means the teacher does not necessarily need to be a master of educational theory and teaching techniques. It makes it more difficult because it means the teacher must live a life that is both worthy of imitation and that inspires imitation.

Why does one identify himself with one person and not another? Why does he accept and follow the attitudes and ideals of this person and not that person? An individual tends to identify himself with and thus learn most from people who are attractive to him. This involves far more than mere physical attractiveness. It refers to that type of person who embodies in an attractive and appealing manner those qualities and ideals which the individual considers desirable and toward which he is striving.

When this concept is applied to the realm of religion, we find, unfortunately, that there are individuals who live perfectly fine Christian lives but who live them in such a way that no one wants to be like them. Perhaps equally unfortunate is the fact that in certain instances those whose lives are most attractive are the ones who have little or no religion. The reason for this is not primarily that the latter engage in "sinful pleasures" which appeal to the fleshly nature of man. The real reason is found in the spirit of the person's life. The attractive person's life is warm and inviting. The Christian life ought to be more attractive than any other type of life. Whether or not it is, depends on the one who is living it.

Our fifth principle, therefore, may be stated: *The Christian teacher should seek to embody the ideals of Christ in such an attractive and winsome way that his life will both be worthy of and inspire imitation.*

IV

SOME DYNAMICS IN THE
TEACHING SITUATION

Teaching does not consist only in techniques and methods. It is not merely a matter of "pushing the right button" and getting the right response. There are dynamic factors in the teaching-learning situation which go beyond technique and method. Dynamics of teaching may be defined as those factors or forces within the teaching-learning situation which cause action, reaction, or interaction. This action, reaction, or interaction may take place within the individual, between the individual and the content, between the individual and the teacher, or between the individual and the group.

A simple example might help make clear what is meant by this definition. A ten-year-old boy has been promoted to a new class. When his teacher walks in the classroom, the boy sees that he has a mustache. The boy has an aversion toward men who wear a mustache. Therefore, there is a reaction on the part of the boy toward the teacher—perhaps unconscious —which, nevertheless, will influence the teaching-learning situation. These dynamics may sometimes cause undesirable reactions, as in the case above, or they may cause desirable reaction. For example, a class of girls may find that they will have as their teacher the most attractive young lady in the church. The girls may react toward the teacher with such enthusiasm that their mind-set for learning will be greatly enhanced.

These dynamic factors in the teaching-learning situation

51

are often difficult to identify. They are also difficult to control. The teacher must be aware of them and seek to control and direct them if he is to have the most favorable learning situation. Actually, anything that is related to the teaching situation, regardless of how trivial, may be a dynamic factor —what type of dress the teacher wears, what happened at home before the learner came to Sunday school, whether the floor is dirty, whether the teacher had a good night's sleep, and so on. Whatever causes action or reaction within or between teacher and learner affects learning. The following discussion will help the teacher identify some of these factors.

Factors That Inhere in the Teacher

The two examples given above illustrate the type of factors which find their source in the teacher. It is probable a majority of these factors will find their source here. What are some others?

Attitude toward the learner.—The teacher's attitude toward the learner is an important factor. Does the teacher respect the learner as a person? Does the teacher indicate a personal interest in the learner? Does his manner and way of teaching indicate he is more interested in the content to be taught than he is in the person to be taught? Does the teacher view the pupils as mere "jugs to be filled"? The members are quick to sense such an attitude on the part of the teacher and to react to it either positively or negatively as the case may be. Has the teacher been able to build up a close personal relationship between himself and his class? This friendly relationship is often built up through contacts between the teacher and members outside of the class session. It is built up through visitation in the home, through social occasions, through personal conferences, through incidental contacts, and in many other ways. Has the teacher been able to lead the members to feel that, as teacher, he understands and fully appreciates their problems, their doubts, their difficulties? He has taken a long step forward toward creating a favorable learning situation if he has developed a close personal relationship with his members.

Attitude toward the material.—The teacher's attitude toward the material to be studied is also significant. If the teacher approaches the lesson in a listless, halting fashion and presents it as though it were dull, dry material that must be covered, the class members will respond in kind. That which is taught must be vital and living in the experience of the teacher if it is to create a favorable reaction within the learner. When the teacher undertakes to teach about forgiveness, about faith, about love for the lost, that truth must be a genuine, integral part of his experience. One reason some teaching leaves the class cold is that it comes from an experiential refrigerator.

Christians in the first century knew little or nothing about psychology or educational principles, but they had an exceedingly effective way of teaching. A part of the reason for their effectiveness was that a burning reality in their experience was that which they taught. They were sharing what they had experienced. When they talked about being courageous in the face of difficulty or forsaking all to follow Christ, they knew what they were talking about, and the "learner" was aware that the "teacher" had experienced it. This is one of the fundamental dynamics of the teaching process.

Attitude toward teaching.—The teacher's attitude toward teaching is also a factor to be considered. For the teacher to conduct his class in a rigid, authoritarian manner may cause an unfavorable reaction on the part of the members which will be a hindrance to their learning. The teacher may have an excellent mastery of the area being studied, he may have planned his lesson with the utmost care, but if the learners react unfavorably to his teaching techniques, the learning that takes place will inevitably be affected.

Does the teacher have a know-it-all attitude in his teaching? This often causes a negative reaction on the part of the learners. While a teacher should seek to be master of his field, it is not expected that he should know everything. The good teacher will sometimes have to say, "I don't know. Let's find out." There must be a willingness to admit limitations but not parade them.

In his teaching, does the teacher seek and appreciate the ideas and experiences of the class members? Is he tolerant of the ideas of others? Is he willing for the class to disagree among themselves and with him without feeling threatened or insecure because of it? Such an attitude may be indicated in this way, "The teacher hasn't acted the same toward me since I disagreed with him on the Christian solution to the moral problem we discussed last month." For a member to react in this way will certainly be a factor in creating for him an unfavorable learning situation.

Personality of the teacher.—The personality of the teacher is also one of the important dynamics in the teaching situation. When one personality comes in contact with another personality, it is inevitable that they will react upon one another in some way, either favorably or unfavorably. This interaction and reaction between teacher and learner has real significance for learning. The teacher may be a fine Christian; he may be a person of high moral character; he may have a good knowledge of the Bible; he may have insight into the best teaching techniques, but if his personality clashes with any or all of his class members, this will be an important factor in determining whether learning will take place. Probably, it will not.

Whatever goes into making what is generally called a "good personality" usually contributes to a favorable learning situation. For example, one is usually attracted to a teacher who has a happy, cheerful disposition and who seeks to make the learning situation a cheerful experience. It is helpful for the teacher to be a relaxed person. Learning usually takes place best in a relaxed, informal situation. The teacher should be a person who has confidence in himself and who inspires confidence in his class members. He should also be a person who has deep convictions about the Christian life but who is not overbearing and dictatorial about his convictions. We usually react favorably to one who knows what he believes and why he believes it, even though we may disagree with him. However, this must be carefully balanced by a tolerance of other people's convictions as mentioned above. Learners usually are attracted to teachers who are approachable. They need to feel that here is a person to whom they can go and talk over their most intimate problems and know that they will find in him a sympathetic and understanding friend. There are many other desirable qualities a teacher should have, but these will serve to point the direction they should take.

Factors That Inhere in the Learner

The teacher is not the only one in the teaching-learning situation who causes action, reaction, and interaction. Certain of these factors find their source in the learner.

The attitude of the learner toward himself—the self concept.—How does the individual view himself? What does he think of himself? What are the central and dominating ideals of his life? What are the goals toward which he is striving? How strong are the drives leading him toward these goals? The attitude of the learner toward himself is of real significance when he comes to the learning situation. For example, there are some young people who have high goals in life. There are others who think no further than next Friday night's date. The ones who will learn best are those who have a vision of what life is all about and who have worthy goals. A teacher may say, "I just can't seem to interest Bill in any way." It may be that Bill has never found himself in life. It may be that his listlessness and indifference is due to the fact that he has no goals, no purposes. He is content to drift because his attitude toward himself and life is one of indifference. It is when the individual has an adequate view of himself, a dominating purpose in life, and a drive within himself sufficient to lead in the direction of that purpose that we have the conditions that are favorable for effective learning.

The attitude of the learner toward the group—the self-other concept.—Another one of the dynamic factors that influences learning is the attitude of the learner toward the group. What does the individual think that the group thinks of him? Whether his interpretation of what the group thinks is correct is beside the point. He reacts to the group on the basis of what he thinks they think. Therefore the question is, does he feel confident in the group? Does he feel that he is accepted or rejected by the group? When the individual thinks those in the learning group will think well of him if he engages in an activity, he will participate and learn. If, on the other hand, the individual feels rejected by the group, then a barrier has been raised in the learning situation which the teacher can overcome only by understanding the situation and meeting it intelligently.

The individual also learns in and from the group whose approval he seeks. It is, therefore, important what he thinks of the church group in general and of his Sunday school class in particular. Are those who compose this group "his" kind, or does he conceive them to be a group of "sissies"? It can easily be seen that one's attitude toward the group might play a significant part in determining whether the learning situation will be favorable or unfavorable.

Closely related to this is the influence of group morale on learning. Studies indicate that in developing attitudes and changing conduct the class spirit plays a significant part. "These habits and attitudes are usually rather specific, however. A case is known, for example, where a whole school developed a sort of taboo against cheating, but extreme snobbishness was condoned if not actually encouraged by the group." [1] This simply re-enforces the thesis of this book that

[1] Carmichael, Leonard, ed., *Manual of Child Psychology* (New York: John Wiley and Sons, Inc., 1946), p. 727.

if we are to secure results from our teaching, we must make our aims much more specific in terms of conduct response.

The attitude of the learner toward the teacher—the self-teacher concept.—The significance of the teacher as a dynamic factor in the teaching-learning situation has been discussed previously. Suffice it to say here that the attitude of the learner toward the teacher may be influenced by matters that are important, or it may be influenced by things that are exceedingly trivial. It may be that the learner does not like the way the teacher combs his hair; it may be that he reacts negatively to the teacher's personality. Important or trivial, whatever it is that determines his attitude provides the psychological environment in which learning must take place whether favorable or unfavorable. It should also be stated that whether the learner's impression of or attitude toward the teacher is correct or not is beside the point so far as it being a dynamic factor in learning is concerned. Whether correct or incorrect, his attitude toward the teacher influences his concept of the learning situation.

The attitude of the learner toward the learning situation—the self-situation concept.—This is another one of those forces which comes into the learning situation without being invited, often without being known, to influence teaching and learning. There are several aspects of this factor that should be identified. First, what is the individual's attitude toward learning in general? Does he have a genuine desire for self-improvement? Whether he does or not will be a partial factor in determining whether he will study and learn in a specific situation.

Second, what is his previous knowledge in the area being studied? Generally the more knowledge a person has in a given area the more interested he is in studying in that area. It may be that the reason he has more knowledge in this area is that he is more interested in it. For example, a person who has no knowledge of electronics might be completely bored by a lecture on that subject while a person who has a good background in the area might be thrilled by the lecture. It may be that one reason some people in our Sunday schools do not show more interest in studying the Bible is that we have not taught them in such a way as to give them a real foundation in Bible knowledge. Perhaps this lack of insight and understanding is one reason for lack of interest on the part of many people.

Third, what is the learner's attitude toward the subject matter being taught? Does he feel that it is "old-fashioned and old fogie?" Does he feel that the Bible presents things that happened so long ago that they have no relation to him? Does he feel that the Sunday school lesson is only to be "talked about" or that it is guidance for life?

The learner is most receptive when, in the learning situation, he reacts, "This is real! This is *my* problem!" Such reaction re-enforces a matter which will be discussed in detail in chapter 9: the importance of making the lesson personal through a life situation or by some other means. Learning takes place best when the learner identifies himself with the situation being studied.

FACTORS THAT INHERE IN THE LEARNING SITUATION

Those factors which find their source in either the teacher or the learner are obviously the most important. However, there are certain factors which inhere in the learning situation itself which must be considered.

Class spirit.—For want of a better term, we refer to one of these factors as "class spirit." The members seem to learn best when there is a strong group spirit and group loyalty. Does each member of the class have a sense of belonging? Is each member of the class accepted by every other member in the class? Has the class developed a strong feeling of "we-ness"? Are there conflicts among the members of the group that hinder the building of a strong class spirit? These conflicts may arise from personal antipathies developed by the members outside of class. They may be caused by social class distinctions or by differences in economic background. Whatever causes differences and distinctions among members, they will tend to be a barrier to learning.

Is there a willingness on the part of the class to take group action? An individual often is more willing to engage in a difficult activity or project as a member of a group than he would be as an individual.

Is there a spirit of freedom and democracy that prevails in the class session? Do the members feel free to express their honest opinions and that neither the other members nor the teacher will censor them for their point of view? This is not easy to achieve. For example, a group of young people may be trying to determine what is the Christian course of action in an "is-it-wrong-to" situation. Some of the members may come to a conclusion that to them seems to be the "higher" or "more Christian" solution. They may, then, tend to develop a holier-than-thou attitude toward those who come to a different conclusion. This can be a vicious and devisive influence in any learning group. The freedom to express one's honest views without fear is essential for effective learning in any teaching situation. Otherwise, the members will simply "answer the teacher's questions" in the way he knows the teacher expects.

Is there a corresponding spirit of authority in the class to balance this spirit of freedom? This is important particularly with groups younger than adults. For a class to have the spirit of freedom and democracy does not mean that the teacher abdicates his position. He must not be so "permissive" as to be "run over" by the class. Children do not respect such a teacher. The teacher is the mature person in the class who not only gives guidance and direction to the learning situation but who also gives control. There must be sufficient authority in the class for the group to understand that their search for spiritual insight and Christian truth is a serious and important undertaking.

Physical factors.—Physical factors, while not necessarily determinative, are often important influences in the learning situation. For example, the matter of ventilation is important. If there is not the proper ventilation and the members become listless and drowsy, their capacity for learning is greatly decreased.

Proper equipment is essential for every age group, but it is particularly important for those who try to teach young children through centers of interest. The teachers of one four-year-old group were struggling along as best they could with poor and inadequate equipment. The church purchased proper equipment for this age group and almost immediately discipline problems vanished and learning was greatly enhanced.

The arrangement of the chairs in the classroom is also significant. It has been pointed out that the traditional arrangement with the teacher at the front and the members seated in rows before him usually leads to a teacher-dominated class. In most instances, the teacher will do most if not all of the talking while the members sit as passive recipients before him. Or the chairs may be arranged in a circle. The teacher takes his place in the circle as a responsible member of the group. In this arrangement everyone faces everyone else. No one is in a position that gives him natural dominance in the situation. This arrangement encourages discussion not only between the teacher and the member but among the members themselves.

Size of class.—The maximum number that should be in a class will vary with the different age groups. In certain groups, there is much discussion today about the relative value of large adult classes and small adult classes. Those who favor the large class emphasize the fellowship that is fostered in the group. The difficulty with this argument is that while the promotion of fellowship is important, fellowship is not the primary purpose of the Sunday school class; teaching is. There are very sound educational principles which would indicate that the small class, even for adults, is better suited for teaching and learning. However, our purpose here is not to discuss the large class versus the small class but to point out some of the dynamics which affect learning that find their source in the size of the class.

The size often affects a person's willingness to participate in the discussion of the lesson. An individual may be exceedingly reluctant to speak out in answer to a question or to express a view in a large class (say of fifty or more). It is so much easier just to keep quiet. Some adult teachers complain that they cannot get their members to discuss the lesson. One reason might be that the class is so large the members are afraid (or embarrassed) to speak out.

For this reason, the size of the class also influences the method of teaching. In a large class, the teacher will almost invariably use the lecture method. There are two reasons for this: The first has already been indicated; he cannot get any of his members to say anything, so he just lectures. The second reason is that the teacher realizes everyone in the class cannot express an opinion, and he does not want to "waste" his time trying to answer the questions they might ask, so—in order to save time and to cover the most material for the most people—he resorts to the lecture method. This practice has real educational significance because, in order for effective learning to take place, the member must be an active participant and not merely a passive listener.

Members also tend to be "lost" in a large class. Most large classes have less than 50 per cent of their enrolment present on any given Sunday. Those who are present fill the room, and the class president says, "We have a good crowd this morning." The 50 per cent who are absent are forgotten and soon become "lost" so far as the class is concerned. While this is a matter of promotion and administration and perhaps has no place in a discussion of dynamics of learning, there is another aspect of this matter that is related.

In a large class a person tends to get "lost" so far as learning is concerned. In those large classes where the teacher has been able to secure some discussion, it should be noted that the ones who speak in class are the same ones, Sunday after Sunday. The majority of the class never say a word. Unconsciously they are "lost"; they sit on the sideline, while the teacher gives his attention to the few who are discussing the lesson. For those who never speak out in a large class, how does the teacher know whether learning has taken place or not? All he can be sure of is that they have been exposed to some teaching, but exposure is not enough.

The Holy Spirit as Teacher

Because we discuss the Holy Spirit as Teacher under the dynamics of learning, it is not to be assumed that we identify him and his work with the psychological actions and interactions of the teaching-learning process. His work is discussed here because it is one of the forces in the teaching situation which goes beyond those matters usually associated with teaching techniques.

It is not the intention here to go into a comprehensive analysis of the biblical teachings of the Holy Spirit as Teacher. Rather, it is our purpose to point out briefly something of his work in the teaching-learning process itself. Two passages in the Gospel of John indicate the teaching function of the Holy Spirit: "These things I have spoken to you, while I am still with you. But the Counselor, the Holy Spirit, whom the Father will send in my name, he will teach you all things, and bring to your remembrance all that I have said to you" (John 14:25–26 RSV). The other passage is even more explicit: "I have yet many things to say to you, but you cannot bear them now. When the Spirit of truth comes, he will guide you into all the truth" (John 16:12–13 RSV). These statements were made to the apostles, but they also apply to all believers (1 John 2:20, 27).

Thus, one of the functions of the Holy Spirit is to lead the Christian into an understanding of truth, that is, to give the seeker Christian insight. "What is truth?" is the perplexing question Pilate asked of Jesus. Today, sincere, earnest Christians are still plagued with problems involving insights as to truth, particularly as it applies to specific life situations. On every side, the questions are heard, "Is it wrong to do this?" "What is right?" "What is the Christian attitude?" The true seeker after the truth, who will diligently search the Scriptures, who will give careful evaluation to all other available help, the Holy Spirit will lead to have insight as to truth.

Another function of the Holy Spirit in the teaching-learning situation is to convict. "And when he comes, he will convince the world of sin and of righteousness and of judgment" (John 16:8 RSV). The basic objective of the teacher is to awaken his members to an awareness of the fact that in certain areas of their lives they are failing to live up to the Christian ideal and to lead them to accept and follow that ideal. Thus the teacher brings to class the problems that the members face in their normal life experiences. What is the Christian attitude toward the underprivileged and how is it to be expressed? What is the Christian attitude toward minority groups and how is it to be expressed? What is the Christian attitude toward the unsaved and how is it to be expressed? What is the Christian attitude in the home and how is it to be expressed? What is the Christian attitude toward society and how is it to be expressed?

Problems such as these are brought before the class for their consideration. In this group discussion, as the Scriptures are searched, as teacher and members together share ideas, insights, and experiences, if one is not living up to the Christian ideal it is in and through this process that the Holy Spirit convicts. This is something the human teacher cannot do. He can present ideas, he can share experiences, but it is the Holy Spirit alone who must convict the individual of any sin or shortcoming in his life.

What teacher among us has not felt keenly his limitations and his inadequacy as he comes to his class with a deep yearning to lead them into some Christian insight, some Christian conviction, some Christian course of action. But after he has done his best there is a point beyond which he cannot pass. At the point of conviction and decision, the teacher stands helpless before the learner. At this point, the Holy Spirit must take over and do his effective work. The teacher can rest assured in the confidence that the Holy Spirit is always present, always ready, always capable of doing his work.

V

STUDYING THE BIBLE
AND THE PUPIL

For a number of years there has been considerable conflict between those who emphasize the content-centered
approach to teaching and those who emphasize the
person-centered approach. One said it was far more important
for the teacher to know the Bible, for teaching without solid
content was mere superficial speculation. The other argued
with equal force that it was far more important for the teacher
to understand the pupil, for teaching without this understanding was mere ineffective exposure.

We are coming to recognize that this argument was fruit-
less as well as unnecessary. There is truth in both positions.
For effective teaching, the teacher must have a mastery of the
Bible knowledge he is to teach. It is equally essential that
he have as full an understanding as possible of the pupil he
teaches. For this reason, the teacher must study both the
Bible and the pupil.

THE TEACHER AND HIS BIBLE

Perhaps it is not necessary among evangelical Christian
groups to stress the unique place of the Bible in Christian education. They recognize that the Bible is central in all Sunday school work. However, we are living in a time when the
philosophy of humanism is running rampant. Man is the
measure of all things. The line between secular and sacred
literature is being wiped out. Man in his arrogant, assump-
tive ignorance is seeking in his own strength to lift himself

to the level of a god. So, perhaps, in such a time as this we need to affirm afresh the unique place of the Bible in Christian education.

The Bible is not a book among books; it is *the* Book among books. It is not one among many source materials; it is the supreme source material. That does not eliminate our use of other books as resources in study and teaching. It simply means that for us who teach religion, the Bible is unique as literature. It is unique in its inspiration, its purpose, its power. It is God's Word to man and, as such, has a unique place in the Sunday school.

Having affirmed the above as a bedrock conviction, perhaps this word of caution is also needed. Although the Bible is unique as the inspired Word of God, it is not a book of magic. Teachers must not assume because they are teaching the Bible that they can merely expose people to it and then expect the Bible to bring about the desired results for which they, as teachers, failed to prepare adequately. They must not expect simply because they are teaching the Bible that children and adults will automatically learn it, love it, and live it. To make such an assumption is to use the Bible in a way God never intended for it to be used. When teachers are sowing the seed of the Word of God, they must follow the suggestion of Jesus that they sow upon good ground that has been properly prepared in order that God might give the increase.

His knowledge of the Bible.—Since the Bible is our central textbook, since it is unique above all books, the teacher must do his best to master it. A teacher's ignorance of the Bible may be one reason pupils know so little of it. The progressive philosophy of education has done us a disservice by minimizing the importance of knowing facts. Bible knowledge is an indispensable part of the teacher's equipment. How can the teacher guide experience, solve problems, answer questions in the realm of Christian attitudes and action unless he has a thorough knowledge of what the

Bible teaches? The Bible knowledge our teachers possess is often so fragmentary that for them to have adequate understanding will call for diligent study. This study is inescapable. For the teacher to fail here is to fail at the very beginning of the teaching-learning process.

His attitude toward the Bible.—Since the Bible is different from all other books, the attitude and response of the teacher to it ought also to be different. Other books, because of their appeal and power, might call forth respect and admiration. But the Bible, because it is the Word of God himself, ought to call from us the attitude of reverent love.

One outstanding religious educator tells how he developed his attitude toward the Bible. He recalled that as a child in a Sunday school class he was inspired by watching how reverently and fondly his teacher handled the Bible. He noted that it was well marked and well used. As each lesson was taught, the Bible was always open and frequently read, not only by the teacher but also by each member of the class. This outstanding educator testified that, not so much from the words of the teacher as from her attitude, he developed a love for the Bible that has grown with the passing years. Pupils can unconsciously tell when a teacher has a genuine love for the Bible. Often the teacher's attitude is his most important asset.

In the fifth and sixth chapters of the Song of Solomon there is an account of a young maiden looking for her beloved. She comes upon a group of young women and requests their help in finding him. The reply is, "Who is thy beloved more than any other beloved that we should seek him?" Then the young maiden describes her beloved in such beautiful and appealing terms that when she finishes, the young women ask, "Where is thy beloved that we too may find him?" In somewhat the same fashion, children, young people, and adults may come to Sunday school and silently say, "What is this Book above any other book that I should study, love, and follow it?" It is then that the teacher must so genuinely love it, study it, live it, and teach it that each member will say, "I want your beloved Book to be a lamp unto my feet and a light unto my pathway—the guide of my life."

His experience of Bible truths.—The Bible is not only a book to be studied, memorized, learned; it is a book to be experienced. Indeed, the Bible is never really learned until it is experienced. One may quote the Scripture verse "It is more blessed to give than to receive," but he does not really know the true meaning of that passage until he has had some experience in sacrificial giving. One may be able to relate the teachings of Jesus about forgiveness but not really know that teaching until he has had some experience in forgiving. One may say, "I die daily" but not know what it really means until he has had the experience of making definite personal sacrifice in which he lays himself on the altar of Christ. One may be able to quote, "The Lord is my shepherd" yet not know the true meaning of this passage until he has had the experience of the Great Shepherd leading him over the dark and rugged way of life.

Therefore, as the teacher studies the Bible, he must be aware that this study is not merely for knowledge but also for life. The teacher must ask himself when preparing each lesson, "What does this lesson mean to me?" He must be certain that the things he undertakes to teach have become a part of his own personal experience. Without this, no teaching can be effective.

The Teacher and His Theology

On the basis of his understanding of the Bible and the Christian faith, the teacher inevitably teaches theology. It is highly important, regardless of the age group being taught, that the teacher be aware of the theology he is teaching and that it has been arrived at on the basis of a careful, intelligent study of the teachings of the Scriptures. What doctrine of God is being taught to the child in the nursery department? Or what view of the church is being taught? One three-year-old child was greatly confused because the teacher constantly referred to the church building as "God's house," but the child complained, "I never see God in his house." What view of prayer is being taught to the child in the Beginner department? Some small children have had their faith in prayer greatly shaken because when they prayed for their grandmother to get well, God didn't "answer" their prayer. What view of Jesus is taught to the Nursery, Beginner, and Primary children?

What view of sin and salvation is being taught to the junior boy or girl? We often seek to lead the children into a personal encounter with Jesus in a conversion experience and to a commitment of their lives to him. How adequately do we help them to understand the meaning of this experience and to understand what is involved in it? What kind of theology do we teach the intermediates and young people? Is it a theology that is both so intelligent and firmly rooted that when they come face to face with conflicting points of view—perhaps in college—they will not be swept off their feet because they have considered these conflicting points of view previously in the Sunday school under the guidance of a Christian teacher?

In some circles, people speak disparagingly of a "Sunday school theology." They mean by this term a theology which is either so superficial and uncritical as to be an ineffective foundation upon which to build a strong superstructure of Christian faith, or a theology that is inaccurate and which later has to be "unlearned," often accompanied by great stress and strain to one's faith. This is not as it should be. Those who are insisting that our children, young people, and adults ought to be more soundly rooted in doctrine (or biblical theology) are calling attention to a matter which has not been given sufficient emphasis in our teaching.

The serious teacher, keenly aware of his own limitations, will be humbled by the seriousness and magnitude of this responsibility. Many teachers are frightened by the very word "theology." They think of it as a technical, highly specialized study for preachers. Indeed, it often is such a study. But there is no necessary cause for alarm and, certainly, no need to be frightened by this area of study. Actually, every Sunday school teacher has his own "theology"; that is, he has views about God, Jesus, the Holy Spirit, the Bible, salvation, baptism, and so forth.

Not only does he have his own theology, he also *teaches* theology. This may come as somewhat of a surprise to some. But Sunday after Sunday as he meets with his class, inevitably and inescapably, he teaches theology in the stories he tells, in the illustrations he uses, in his answers to questions, in the statements he makes. It is not a question of teaching theology or not teaching theology. Rather, it is a question of whether the theology which he teaches has, like Topsy, "just growed up" and been accepted uncritically, or whether it is soundly based in the Bible and has been critically examined by the teacher and consciously accepted on the basis of, at least, some diligent study and reasoned reflection.

The average Sunday school teacher protests that he is not capable of giving this kind of instruction to his class members. How shall the teacher of small children interpret the experience of death to them when some pet has died or when some relative or friend has passed away? How shall they interpret the meaning of life after death accurately and meaningfully in terms of the child's own experience? How shall the teacher of older children, young people, and adults interpret the doctrine of the church, the doctrine of the Holy Spirit, the doctrine of the inspiration of the Scriptures and the other great doctrines of our faith to those whom they teach? This is but to point out again the pressing need for our teachers to engage in serious, directed study of the Bible. Admittedly, theirs is a responsibility of no small magnitude, and they are only volunteer lay leaders. They have never had the opportunity for specialized theological study in a seminary. They, themselves, would like to have their own faith clarified and deepened. They would like to be able to give to those whom they teach a sound basis for Christian faith. But to whom shall they turn to receive this guidance for themselves, first?

They could request the pastor or minister of education to guide them in this study. (Incidentally, this is one of the reasons it is necessary for the minister of education to have a thorough theological training as well as a sound foundation in educational principles and methods.) What greater service can the pastor or minister of education render his teachers than to lead them in a serious study of the fundamentals of our faith? It is readily apparent that it would be an unfortunate and serious matter for a conflict to exist between the theology that is preached in the pulpit and that taught in the Sunday school classroom. If any such conflict does exist, it may be that it is purely unintentional. It may be that the teacher is not aware of the theological implications of the things he is teaching, because he has never been led in a careful consideration of these matters.

How can this instruction be given to the teachers? The regular training courses the church offers for teacher-training can certainly be used. Several excellent denominational books may be available. For instance, Southern Baptists use the Training Course Series.[1] This study may also be undertaken in the regular prayer meeting, for it would be of benefit to the entire congregation. Or, it may be done, for a specified number of weeks, in the study period of the weekly officers and teachers' meeting. All of the teachers could meet together in one group for this study; although when this is done the teachers do not get specific guidance for teaching next Sunday's lesson, and that is what they seem to desire

[1] Mullins, E. Y. and Tribble, H. W., *The Baptist Faith;* White, W. R., *Baptist Distinctives;* Wallace, O. C. S., *What Baptists Believe;* Tribble, H. W., *Our Doctrines.* Others that will be helpful are: Conner, W. T., *Revelation and God, The Gospel of Redemption;* Payne, E. H., *The Fellowship of Believers;* Robinson, H. W., *The Life and Faith of the Baptists, Baptist Principles;* Torbet, R. G., *A History of the Baptists.*

most. However, for a matter of such significance as this, it might be well for the teachers to concentrate for a time on the theology they teach. Or, this study may be done on a departmental basis. In the preview study for the quarter, the teachers may be led in a consideration of the theological implications of the lessons to be taught during the quarter.

The church library will be a valuable aid in providing materials for study in this area. Books of a non-technical nature dealing with theology should be secured by the church library for use by both teachers and class members. When and how this study should be done will have to be determined by each individual situation, but give this help to our teachers we must.

It is necessary to add this further word. It is entirely possible—even probable—that there will not be unanimity of agreement concerning these matters of doctrine on the part of all the teachers. We believe that each individual is competent to study the Scriptures for himself and that, under the leadership of the Holy Spirit, he should be left free to come to his own conclusions. The only thing we are trying to emphasize here is that the teacher's theology should be consciously accepted on the basis of a careful and serious study of the Bible.

THE TEACHER STUDYING HIS BIBLE

Stimulating teachers in Bible study.—Perhaps a word should be said here to pastors, ministers of education, and others who may have responsibility for teacher training. To say that teachers ought to study the Bible is merely to state the problem. It certainly does not solve it. These teachers are volunteer, lay workers. They are insurance men, farmers, grocerymen, laborers, lawyers, housewives, stenographers, receptionists, and others. They have families to support and care for. They have a living to make. They have other responsibilities and interests. They know they ought to study the Bible more, but for one reason or another they have not done so. How can we stimulate our teachers to study? There is no easy answer to this question. The following are given as suggestive:

1. Arouse in them a genuine desire to take their task of teaching seriously.

2. Impress upon them afresh the basic importance of mastering the content and meaning of the Bible. The theological matters which we have just discussed will help them to become more aware of this need.

3. Lead the teachers to face the fact of their lack of Bible knowledge. One way to do this is to lead them to take some objective Bible knowledge tests. The teachers can check their own papers, and no one else need ever know what grade the teacher makes. Or, if the teachers are properly prepared, these Bible knowledge tests can be given without the above precaution being taken.

4. Provide an intensive program of publicity in the church for Bible study.

5. Observe a week of Bible study each year. (Southern Baptists have a Bible Study Week the first week in January each year.)

6. Provide Bible study for your teachers and others in prayer meeting.

7. Provide definite materials or books for teachers to use in Bible study at home.

8. Each quarter lead the teachers in a preview study covering the lessons for the next quarter.

9. Use motion pictures and other visual aids that are based on Bible materials.

10. Provide a good church library and encourage your teachers to use it.

11. Encourage your teachers to attend associational, state, and Southwide conferences.

Helping the teachers know how to study the Bible.—If the teacher is going to study his Bible properly, it must not be done in a haphazard fashion or in an incidental manner.

It must be done on a systematic basis, or it probably will not be done at all. Therefore, the teacher should have a definite time for Bible study.

It should be understood that this study is not to be confused with or take the place of one's own personal daily devotions. It is for the teacher to determine whether this systematic study of the Bible is to be done every day or every other day. He must decide how much time is to be spent in each study period and determine at what time of the day it is to be done. The important thing is that a definite time be set and used faithfully for Bible study.

One or two things should be kept in mind in determining the time. It should be a period when everything will be quiet, and it should be an uninterrupted study. One cannot study the Bible properly if the telephone is ringing or if the children are making too much noise about the house or if there are other interruptions. Therefore each teacher must determine for himself the best time to be allotted for his Bible study.

Because of the variety of the material, teachers who begin a study of the Bible need a plan to follow.[2] They must know what they are going to study and how and why they are going to study it. Besides the theological approach suggested earlier, there are several other possibilities from which to choose. For example, the teacher might study the Bible according to the *lesson passages* suggested in the Sunday school quarterly. He will, of course, include the Scripture suggestions in the "larger lesson" for each week's study. If this plan is followed, the teacher will soon find that he has more material than he can possibly use on Sunday. Thus his teaching will begin to reflect the "overflow."

The teacher might choose the plan of studying the Bible *extensively*. In this plan, one seeks to obtain a comprehensive view of the Bible. Just as an individual often cannot see the

[2] Dobbins, G. S., *The Improvement of Teaching in the Sunday School* (Nashville: Broadman Press, 1943), pp. 41–48. Used by permission.

forest for the trees, a teacher misses the meaning and message of the Bible in its entirety because he deals almost exclusively with its parts. Thus he often fails to grasp and appreciate the essential unity of the Scriptures. The teacher might follow an outline similar to the following:

Major events from Abraham to Moses

Major events from Moses to the Conquest of Canaan

Major events from the Conquest of Canaan to the Divided Kingdom

Major events in the Northern Kingdom to the Exile

Major events in the Southern Kingdom to the Exile

Major events from the return from Exile to the building of the second Temple

As the teacher studies the major events in these various periods, he watches God as he takes his majestic steps across the mountain peaks of religious history. This type of study enables one to see, clearly and realistically, God at work in human affairs.[3]

A third plan is to make an *intensive* study of the Bible. This plan is exactly opposite from the plan suggested above. Instead of trying to comprehend the Bible in its broad, general aspects the teacher selects, perhaps, one book and gives himself to an intensive study of that particular portion. If the teacher chose to study the Gospel of Luke, he would want to study something about the time it was written, the author, the social and political situation in which it was written, its purpose, its major teachings. He would then make a study of the book itself, paragraph by paragraph, and sometimes even word by word.

Many have found the study of the Bible by *characters* to be rewarding. In this plan, the teacher selects a group of the great Bible personalities and studies all of the biblical refer-

[3] The following are some books that might be helpful to the teacher who desires to follow this plan of Bible study: Tribble, H. W., *From Adam to Moses;* Hill, J. L., *From Joshua to David;* Yates, K. M., *From Solomon to Malachi;* Moore, H. C, *From Bethlehem to Olivet* and *From Pentecost to Patmos.*

ences relating to these particular persons. In this way he comes to live intimately with such men as Moses, Isaiah, Saul, Solomon, David, Jeremiah, Peter, John, Mark, and Paul. He comes to see more clearly their problems, their struggles, their failures, their triumphs. From this type of study, the teacher will get a wealth of illustrations to enrich his teaching.

If any of these plans are followed, the teacher will need some study helps to guide him. Excellent, yet inexpensive, commentaries and other helps are available. Contact your denominational book store.

A word of caution and encouragement should be given at this point. To follow a systematic plan of Bible study is not easy. Temptations to give it up (or not to start) and interference will come on every hand. There is work to be done at the office; there are meals to be cooked; there are clothes to be washed; there are meetings to be attended. And, as the teacher is "busy here and there," the Bible study is neglected. However, one does not become proficient in Bible knowledge simply by accident. Neither will wishing make it so. Insight into and understanding of the Scriptures come only by long, hard hours of diligent study. To many, it may seem a high price to pay, but it pays rich dividends both in the enrichment of the teacher's personal life and in his increased ability to enrich the lives of those whom he teaches.

THE TEACHER AND THE PUPIL

It would be difficult to place too great an emphasis on knowing the Bible, but, in the final analysis, Bible knowledge is primarily a means to an end. The ultimate objective is that the individual appropriate this knowledge in such a way that he will express it in his daily relationships. In this way, there is a proper balance between the subject and the object of teaching, between knowledge and life, between the Bible and the pupil.

One without the other is incomplete. The pupil is at the

center of the learning process, but his experience must be analyzed, evaluated, and directed in terms of the Bible and the Christian heritage. If modern progressive education did us a disservice by minimizing the importance of knowing facts, it rendered us an invaluable service in leading us to place a greater emphasis upon understanding the learner.

What did Jesus mean when he said, "The sabbath was made for man, and not man for the sabbath" (Mark 2:27)? Surely he must have meant that no religious observance, rite, or ceremony—regardless of how sacred it may seem to be— is to supersede human personality in importance. Sunday school teachers need to learn this truth. In spite of all of the efforts of Sunday school leaders to the contrary, far too often teachers let lessons become of more importance than the pupil in the teaching situation. In too many instances, the pupil exists for the lesson rather than the lesson existing for the pupil. It is essential that the teacher have a deep appreciation of the importance of the pupil in the teacher-learner process.

Everything that exists in the Sunday school exists for the sake of class members. Buildings are built, money is spent, literature is written, teachers are enlisted, prospects are discovered, a visitation program is engaged in, energy is expended, the Bible is taught—all for the sake of people that they might have life and have it abundantly. Like Jesus, we must place the child in the midst and let the child (or the class member) determine everything that is done in the Sunday school. If we may paraphrase this statement of Jesus, we might say "The Sunday school was made for man and not man for the Sunday school."

JESUS' CONCERN FOR PERSONS

One of the unique revelations of Jesus concerned the worth of individuals. He held that each individual was of infinite worth. Whether the individual was the rich young ruler or the woman taken in adultery, whether it was Nicodemus or the Samaritan woman—or, in modern terms, whether it was the son of a mayor or one of the dead-end-kids from the other side of the tracks—each individual was of supreme importance.

The ministry of Jesus was a person-minded ministry. The particular needs of the individual largely determined his approach, his content, and his method. To the rich young ruler, who, in haughty pride was seeking to find a righteousness within himself, Jesus said, "Go and sell that thou hast and give to the poor" (Matt. 19:21). But to the woman taken in adultery—already slapped by society and needing to know that there was someone who believed in her enough to give her a chance—Jesus said, "Neither do I condemn thee; go, and sin no more" (John 8:11). Recall how Jesus dealt with his problem disciples, with James and John and the angry disciples, with vacillating Peter, with doubting Thomas. He gave to them all the same soul-saving message, but the need of each individual determined what he gave and how he gave it.

Someone may object, "It is so important that our members learn the Bible." That is true but we must remember that Jesus came with the greatest message the world has ever known. He did not try to teach that message in "package form." He knew that merely to expose people to his great truths would not necessarily mean that they would learn them or experience them. He recognized that the pupil, his interests and his needs, must determine what is taught and how it is taught. Recognizing this supremely important educational principle, Jesus, on one occasion, said, "I have yet many things to say unto you, but ye cannot bear them now" (John 16:12).

Looking at this through purely human eyes, what a temptation this must have been to Jesus! Picture the situation. There he was, the divine Son of God with all his wisdom and insight concerning God, the kingdom of God, life after death, forgiveness, righteousness, and all the rest. Time was so short! Soon he would no longer walk with his disciples in the flesh. There they were. He was depending so heavily upon them to carry on his work. There was so much they needed to know! Surely, we would have been tempted to give them systematic lectures on God, salvation, forgiveness, ethics, and all the other important matters they needed to know.

Jesus knew that exposure to this knowledge was not enough. If they were to learn these spiritual truths in their experience (the only way that Christian truth has any meaning!) he had to teach them in light of and in terms of their background, their needs, their interests. His "curriculum"— that is, what he taught—was conditioned by his learners. If this was the method of Jesus, teachers today can do no better than follow his example.

The Teacher Understanding the Pupil

Teachers must come to a fresh consciousness of the infinite worth of each individual and to a new awareness of the importance and centrality of the pupil in the teacher-learner process. "A teacher does not teach a class or group. He works with *individuals,* who may gather at times in classes or groups. Each individual is unique in God's sight. He should be so in the teacher's sight." [4]

Just how well does the teacher know and understand each of his class members? He may know their names, addresses, ages, birthdays. How much more does he know? Does he have an understanding and appreciation of each one as a person? Does he feel that because his members need what the Bible teaches the best thing for him to do is tell them what it says and what it means irrespective of their individual interests and their particular needs?

Of course, all the members need what the Bible teaches. But each member is an individual whose life, hopes, dreams, experiences, problems must be understood; and, being understood, must be directed in harmony with the ideals of the

[4] Bowman, Clarice M., *Ways Youth Learn* (New York: Harper and Brothers, 1952), p. 45. Used by permission.

Christian faith. The following testimony of a high school teacher ought to cause every earnest Christian teacher to pause and examine his own teaching:

> I have taught in high school for ten years. During that time I have given assignments, among others, to a murderer, an evangelist, a pugilist, a thief, and an imbecile.
> The murderer was a quiet little boy who sat on the front seat and regarded me with pale blue eyes; the evangelist, easily the most popular boy in the school, had the lead in the junior play; the pugilist lounged by the window and let loose at intervals a raucous laugh that startled even the geraniums; the thief was a gay-hearted Lothario with a song on his lips; and the imbecile, a soft-eyed little animal seeking the shadows.
> The murderer awaits death in the state penitentiary; the evangelist has lain a year now in the village churchyard; the pugilist lost an eye in a brawl in Hong Kong; the thief, by standing on tiptoe, can see the window of my room from the county jail; and the once gentle-eyed little moron beats his head against a padded wall in the state asylum.
> All of these pupils once sat in my room, sat and looked at me gravely across worn brown desks. I must have been a great help to those pupils—I taught them the rhyming scheme of the Elizabethan sonnet and how to diagram a complex sentence.[5]

How many times this may have happened in our Sunday schools we do not know. In every class there are those who have problems. Not all of the problems are as acute as those mentioned above, but they are problems nevertheless. Children, young people, and even adults are often confused, perplexed, and puzzled. Silently they cry out, "Don't you see, I need help!" But so often the teacher goes on blindly teaching "the lesson" in the vague hope that he is "doing some good." It is not enough for the teacher to have a vague hope. Human lives and eternal destinies hang in the balance! He must know the members of his class so intimately that he can teach them in light of their problems and their needs.

[5] Quoted in Schorling, Raleigh, *Student Teaching* (New York: McGraw-Hill Book Co., Inc., 1940), p. 47.

INFORMATION THE TEACHER NEEDS

Since this is true the teacher must give as much diligence to the task of studying and understanding each of his members as he does to studying and understanding the lesson he teaches. One of the first things he will need to do is to get a general understanding of the age group he teaches. Those in any age group will have certain characteristics in common. For example, the average class of adolescents will display ways of thinking and acting that are common to almost any group of adolescents. This information will enable the teacher to know what to expect in general from his members.

On the other hand, the teacher must recognize that this general information does not give him specific understanding of Tom, Jack, or Bill. While they have certain characteristics in common, they also have individual differences of backgrounds, interests, problems, needs. Parents are often amazed at the difference in two children of the same family. They have the same parents; they have been reared in the same environment with the same training. Yet they are entirely different. What works with one will have no effect on the other. Parents have found that to try to deal with their children in the same way is often sheer folly. Just so, the teacher must come to recognize and understand the individual differences that exist in his class members and minister to them in light of their own particular individuality.

A rather comprehensive list of questions is given below to serve as a guide for the teacher in knowing the type of information that should be secured. Not all questions will apply to all age groups. The teacher will select those that seem best to serve his purpose. Undoubtedly, he will add questions of his own which are not included here.

1. GENERAL INFORMATION

Name _____ Address _____

Telephone number _____ Birth date _____ Age _____
    Sex _____

Department _____ Class _____

2. HOME LIFE

Father's name? _____ Occupation? _____.

Church member? _____ Where? _____ Sunday school
  member? _____

Mother's name? _____ Occupation? _____

Church member? _____ Where? _____ Sunday school
  member? _____

Brothers? _____ Name and age of each? _____

Church member? _____ Where? _____ Sunday school
  member? _____

Sisters? _____ Name and age of each? _____

Church member? _____ Where? _____ Sunday school
  member? _____

What is his attitude toward other members of the family? _____

Do they have family worship? _____ Does the child participate?
_____

Does the child have assigned daily chores? _____ What is his attitude
  toward them? _____

What is his attitude toward discipline? _____

What is the economic status of the family? _____

Is there an atmosphere of love and happiness in the home? _____

What are the attitudes of the father and mother toward the child?
_____

Do they display a keen interest in the child? _____ Would the
  neighborhood be rated as above average, average, or below average? _____ What unfavorable influences are there in the
  community? _____

What favorable influences? _____

3. SCHOOL LIFE

Name of school? _____ Name of teacher? _____

Grade? _____ Attitude toward school? _____

Attitude toward teacher? _____

General grades? _____ What subject does he like best? _____

Dislike? _____ What extra-curricula activities does he engage in? _____ Does he like to read? _____

Does he use library facilities? _____ What books does he read?
_____

Is he on the athletic teams? _____ What is his social relationship
  with others in his school? _____

4. COMPANIONSHIPS

Does he have few or many friends? _____ Does he make friends
  readily or slowly? _____ Is he concerned more to give or to
  get in friendships? _____ Is the influence of his companions
  in general helpful or harmful? _____ Is he primarily a leader
  or a follower? _____

Does he choose his companions from the same social level or otherwise? _____ From church circle or elsewhere? _____
What evidences of growth in capacity for Christian friendship? _____

5. TEMPERAMENT AND DISPOSITION

Is he primarily self-centered or interested in others? _____
Is he sensitive? _____ Is he good natured? _____ Is he dependent or independent? _____ Does he like notice and prominence? _____ Does he shrink from responsibility? _____
Is he more aggressive or timid? _____
Does he have a happy outlook on life? _____ Does he have a healthy attitude toward religion? _____ Does he anger easily? _____
Does he control his temper and emotions? _____ Is he able to reason? _____ Does he have a cheerful disposition? _____ Is he tolerant of others? _____

6. RECREATION AND HOBBIES

What is his favorite recreational activity? _____ What other types of recreation does he engage in? _____ How much time does he have for recreation? _____ Does he play well with others? _____ Does he enter actively into sports? _____ Does he follow sports primarily as a spectator? _____
What hobbies does he have? _____
What type of social life does he engage in? _____
Is he more of a leader or a follower in recreation? _____

7. SPECIAL INTERESTS AND ABILITIES

Indicate interests that center chiefly about the home. _____
About work. _____ About school. _____
About intellectual activities. _____ About social activities. _____ Indicate his interest in the home. _____ His interest in money making. _____ His interest in crafts. _____ Arts. _____ Music.

What does he talk about being when he grows up? _____
What are his talents? _____ How is he using them? _____ Does he need help in developing them? _____ What is his attitude toward his talents? _____ Is he afraid of criticism? _____

8. RELIGIOUS LIFE

Is he a Christian? _____ Church member? _____ What services of the church does he attend? _____
What services seem most to appeal to him? _____
In what organized activities of the church does he take part? _____

Is he interested in or indifferent to Bible study? _____

Is he interested in or indifferent to his church? _____ Is his
religion an annoyance, a duty, a habit, or a source of joy? _____

Is his religion a growing, developing part of his life? _____

Does he put into practice what he learns in Sunday school and
church? _____

Is he interested in missions? _____ Does he seek to enlist others?
_____

What is his attitude toward stewardship? _____.

Is he a personal witness? _____

Present religious development.—It is difficult to state in
terms of questions the information the teacher needs concerning the present religious development of each member.
Yet, in order for the teachers to meet the individual needs of
each member, this information is the most important of all.

The teacher should know the learner's present religious
knowledge. If one of the teacher's tasks is to eliminate ignorance, then he must know what that ignorance is. Good teaching must begin at the level of the learner's present understanding. It may be that the teacher is teaching far beyond
the present knowledge of his members and they sit and listen, perhaps not even knowing enough to ask a question. Or
it may be that the teacher is dealing with the Bible material
on such an elementary level the members are bored with the
class session. One of the tasks of the teacher is to teach the
Bible, but in order to do this he must know the present level
of the learner's religious knowledge in the area being
studied.

Even more important the teacher must know the learner's
present religious attitudes.[6] Through understanding the pupil's present attitudes, the teacher discovers his religious
problems and needs. What is his attitude toward God? What
is his attitude toward the church? What is his attitude toward
the Bible? What is his attitude toward prayer? What is his attitude toward minority groups? What is his attitude toward

[6] The child's present religious attitudes may be discovered by private,
informal conversations, by observing his comments in class, and through in-
terviews with his parents.

the foreigner in his school? After getting the answers to questions like these, the teacher becomes aware of the particular needs of each member in his class. If the teacher has a lesson on prayer, he must remember that Larry, Hoyt, and Jimmie are in the class. The need of each one relative to prayer may be different. Through knowing their attitude toward prayer, he knows in advance the particular need of each, and he can plan his lesson in such a way that the need of each will be met. How different this is from teaching a lesson in general on prayer and hoping the members will get something out of it. One way the teacher might use to get this information concerning the pupil's religious attitudes is suggested in chapter XIII under the heading "Quarterly Parent Interview."

How to Get and Use This Information

As the teacher looks over these suggested questions, he immediately asks, "How can I ever get all this information?" It is not nearly as difficult as it might seem at first glance. Indeed, those who have undertaken to do this have found it such an enlightening and rewarding experience that the time and effort involved is negligible. All of this information will not be secured at once. It will be gathered over a period of weeks and months as the teacher observes the members of the class. Here are some suggestions that might prove helpful.

How to get this information.—First, study some books about the particular age group. This will give the teacher a general background and help him know what to look for. There are many good books written in popular style that will help the teacher understand the psychology of the age group he teaches.

Second, much of this information can be secured through the use of a suitable questionnaire which the pupils are asked to fill out. Of course, the teacher will have to select only those questions which are appropriate for a pupil questionnaire. He could use such questions as: What subject do you like most in school? Which one do you like least? What are your hobbies? He would not include questions that are too personal in nature, such as: Are you sensitive? self-centered? and so on. The members can be asked to fill out such a mimeographed questionnaire after they have been promoted to the class. In this way, the teacher will have much valuable information about each member at the beginning of the year. This will also serve as a good foundation upon which to build as the teacher secures other information. The class members will not resent being asked to fill out such a questionnaire. It is more likely they will be highly pleased to know that the teacher is interested in them to this extent.

Information may be secured also as the teacher visits in the home with the members of his class. He does not go with the intent of prying into other people's affairs, but he has merely to keep his eyes and ears open to gain much helpful information. In personal conversations with the pupil before or after Sunday school, or as they meet on the street or have a soda together, the teacher will get insight as to his interests and attitudes.

Special conferences with the parents would be helpful. This is an area that has not been developed sufficiently. There is great profit to be found in the parent and Sunday school teacher working closely with each other in the religious training of the child. If the teacher is able to develop the right kind of relationship with the parent, he will find this to be his best source of information as well as assistance.

The teacher will be able to add to his store of information through observation. As he engages in social activities with the group, as he watches the group play together, and in many other ways helpful information will come to him. The important thing is for the teacher to become "information conscious" so that he will be constantly on the lookout for these insights. When he hears or sees something that is significant, he must be sure to write it down in his pupil information notebook. The teacher is not to try to be a little psychiatrist. But all of us are constantly doing things which say "I need help in this area" or "My attitude and conduct are not Christian in this area." It is the task and privilege of the Christian teacher to meet the needs of each of his members, if only he has eyes to see.

How to keep this information.—What is the best way to keep this information about the class members? That will depend largely on the individual preference of the teacher. One good way is to keep it in a loose-leaf notebook. The questions should be mimeographed on regular size paper. Be sure to leave sufficient space between certain questions so that information may be added under the question when it is obtained. This will mean that the teacher will have several pages in the notebook for each member. It would make the information much more personal if the teacher would secure a picture of each member of his class and attach it to the first page of the information dealing with each member.

How to use this information.—The information that has thus been secured by the teacher is indispensable in teaching every lesson. The teacher should study the information concerning his members as diligently as he studies the Bible to find out the important things in the lesson. This data may be used in each step of the lesson plan. In selecting an aim for a given lesson, the teacher will study the information he has on each member to discover their needs, their problems, and their present attitudes in the area to be studied. In this way, he will be able to make his lesson aim much more personal and much more specific. In stimulating interest for purposeful Bible study, he will be able to appeal to the normal interests which the members have indicated they have.

This information will be particularly helpful in developing the lesson. In one part of the lesson discussion, the teacher may bring out a particular point because that is what one member needs. In another part of the discussion, he can ask a question or use an illustration that will illuminate some point another member needs. Thus, the development of the lesson can be adapted to meet the specific need of each member in the class. When the teacher comes to the next step in the lesson plan, he will find that it is far easier to relate the spiritual truth to normal experience of his members if he knows some of the problems they are now facing in that particular area. In securing carry-over, he will find in this information suggestions as to ways in which the member would be able to express in life the spiritual truth that is being studied.

This may seem to the teacher to be an involved and difficult task, but it should also be apparent to him that in following such a procedure there is much more likelihood he will secure *results* from his teaching than if he taught only in generalized terms. For him to know his pupils intimately and teach them in light of their personal problems and needs is to follow the example of Jesus, the Master Teacher.

VI

MAKING AIMS SPECIFIC

Many teachers ask, "How shall I go about preparing my lesson for Sunday? Is there an outline or lesson plan to give me guidance?" The next five chapters will try to help the teacher answer these questions. In them, we will give a rather detailed discussion of the various divisions of a lesson plan the teacher may use in preparing and teaching a lesson. Each division of the plan here suggested will be related to a principle of teaching which, if followed, might play an important part in making teaching more effective. The divisions of the lesson plan and the principles to be discussed are as follows:

1. How to state an aim: The teacher must state an aim in terms of knowledge, inspiration, or conduct response, depending upon the type of results he desires to achieve. The aim must be sufficiently specific that there is the possibility of achieving definite results.

2. How to secure purposeful Bible study: In introducing the lesson the teacher must arouse interest or curiosity on the part of the class members before there will be a purposeful study of the Bible.

3. How to develop the lesson: In developing the lesson the teacher should seek to lead the class to an understanding of the Christian attitude being studied. He should use only that material which will contribute to the achieving of his aim.

4. How to make the lesson personal: The teacher must lead the class to see how the spiritual truth under consideration would apply or operate in one of their normal life situations.

5. How to secure carry-over: Plans for carry-over should be made in the class session.

Suggestions will also be given as to how these five principles may be developed into a workable lesson plan. The importance of these principles cannot be stressed too greatly.

A WEAKNESS

If we are going to secure results from our teaching, we must know the specific results we desire. In too many instances teachers study their lesson, perhaps carefully, getting a general idea of what it is about. They may even plan a good outline of it. But they teach it on Sunday in general terms only. Seemingly, their primary objective is "to teach the lesson." Herein lies a major weakness. They do not have a specific objective in mind. If some Sunday morning the Sunday school superintendent should meet his teachers at the front of the church and ask them the question "What is your aim for the lesson this morning?" some would look at him with open-mouth amazement. Some would question, "What do you mean?" Many would be seriously embarrassed because they could not respond. Some would give a generalized aim such as, "My aim is to teach the Bible," or "My aim is to develop Christian character." Probably very few would be able to give a valid statement of a good aim. This is one of the most tragic aspects of our teaching today. Teaching the living Word of God to human beings is far too important to have this kind of aimless teaching.

As a result of this lack of aims on the part of the teacher, there are some unfortunate consequences that attend the teaching. For example, the teacher tries to cover too much material. Since he has no aim or objective in mind, he has no basis by which to determine what part of the lesson material should be selected and what part of necessity has to be omitted and, in trying to cover too much material, actually accomplishes little.

He will also have a tendency to ramble in his teaching.

Having no definite goal in mind to guide him on his way, the teacher is tempted to go down side streets and waste his time on non-essentials, skipping from one topic to another. Perhaps one of the most serious consequences is that the teaching will often be unrelated to life needs. The teacher, not having given sufficient care in preparation to secure a definite aim, merely talks. The problems of the class members that are begging for solution remain untouched and unsolved.

Finally, there probably will be little or no results from this type of aimless teaching. The likelihood is there will be neither definite changes in attitude nor in conduct because the teacher had none in mind. Dr. G. S. Dobbins is fond of quoting a saying by Hambone: "One reason some folks don't git no whar is dat dey wo'nt gwin' no whar in de fust place."

What Is an Aim?

Dr. Paul H. Vieth says, "An objective [or aim] is a statement of a result consciously accepted as a desired outcome of a given process." [1] In less technical language, an aim is simply a statement of that which the teacher hopes to accomplish. Professor Dewey says, "Acting with an aim is all one with acting intelligently." [2] Having an aim lifts the teaching process to the level of consciousness, intelligence, and purpose.

The teacher may be perplexed as to how he should go about trying to work out an aim. What factors should be considered in determining an aim? First of all, there is the lesson that the teacher is dealing with on a given Sunday. Second, life must be considered. Someone has said that one of the tasks of education is to help people do better what they are going to have to do anyway. What are some of the problems people face? What are some of the decisions they must make?

[1] Vieth, Paul H., *Objectives in Religious Education* (New York: Harper and Brothers, 1930), p. 18.

[2] Dewey, John, *Democracy and Education* (New York: The Macmillan Company, 1923), p. 120.

Sunday school teachers should seek always to have their aims closely related to life.

Third, the members of the class must also be carefully considered. Life tells the teacher many things in general, but the teacher is not teaching a group in general; he is teaching a particular class. Thus his aims must be determined by the specific needs of the members of his specific class. The teacher's notebook, suggested earlier, with detailed information concerning the members of his class will be exceedingly helpful in determining what those specific needs are and in determining what his aims should be. The more complete and accurate this notebook, the more helpful it will be to the teacher. The wise teacher will search the suggested Scripture carefully and find the aim which most closely corresponds to the deepest needs of his class members.

Qualities of a Good Aim

How may the teacher know whether the aim he has selected is a good aim or not? The following are some qualities which he might use to test his aim:

It ought to be brief enough to be remembered.—When the teacher does state an aim, too many times it is long, involved, and complex. The aim is the statement of what the teacher wants a class to learn or do. If the statement is so long that the teacher cannot remember it, how can he expect the class to practice it? Therefore, it should be brief enough to be remembered, and the teacher should be able to quote it without difficulty.

It ought to be clear enough to be written down.—Another difficulty that teachers often have as they try to give a statement of aim is to make it clear. The teacher feels that he has the aim clearly in his own mind, but when he tries to state it, he finds that he is confused and usually ends up by saying, "Oh, you know what I mean." Many times, we may think an aim is clear to us until we try to write it. Then we find it exceedingly difficult to express exactly what we mean. We must conclude that it is not a good aim unless it is clear enough to be written down.

It ought to be specific enough to be achieved.—One of the major weaknesses in this problem is that our aims have been too vague and too general. The teacher must recognize that on a given Sunday he will have only thirty minutes in which to teach. In stating an aim for that lesson, he ought to try to make it specific enough to achieve within the time limits of the class session. This point will be discussed more fully later.

The question is often asked, "Should the aim be stated to the class?" It depends on the type of aim the teacher has in mind. If he is seeking a knowledge aim it would be quite all right to state it. But if he has an inspiration or conduct response aim in mind it is probably neither wise nor helpful for the teacher at the beginning of the class session to say "My aim for this lesson is thus and so." As the teacher teaches the lesson the aim should be so clear in the lesson that the class members will be well aware of it. When the session is over if someone were to ask a member "What was your teacher's aim this morning?" the member ought to be able to reply without hesitation.

Types of Aims

When we consider teaching as it is done in the Sunday school, we usually think of three types of aims. They are:

Quarterly aims.—This, of course, refers to the aim that the teacher may have for the series of lessons to be studied in a given quarter. This type of aim is often referred to as a general aim. Since a general aim might also refer to an aim for a year or even for life, it seems that the sake of clarity will better be served by the use of the more specific term quarterly aim.

If the teacher is going to secure results from his teaching, it will be necessary for him to have a clear and definite aim for the quarter. This means that the teacher will have to study all of the lessons for the next quarter in order to determine what objectives he desires to reach in the lives of his class members through these lessons. The teacher may say that this is too difficult and takes too much time, but it is absolutely necessary to have unity and purpose in his teaching efforts and in order to obtain results.

Too many teachers teach each lesson as a unit in itself, unrelated to the lesson that was taught last Sunday and unrelated to the lesson that will be taught next Sunday. If we were to try to picture this kind of teaching, the lessons would look something like this:

In these lessons, the class activity is headed in some direction —but where? With this kind of teaching, there is often little or no sense of achievement or accomplishment at the end of the quarter. The class has just been led to cover a series of isolated and unrelated lessons.

When the teacher has an aim for the quarter he is able to see how each lesson will contribute to its accomplishment. In this way the foundation of each lesson is built on the preceding lesson and leads to the one that is to follow. If we were to try to picture this type of teaching, it might look somewhat as follows:

Actually, this picture will be changed when we consider unit aims. When the teacher has a clear aim for the quarter in mind, each lesson is related to every other lesson and each lesson contributes its part to the achieving of the quarterly aim. At the end of the quarter, there is a sense of achievement both on the part of the class members and on the part of the teacher. The point being made here is very simple. The teacher will have a far better chance of achieving results in increased Bible knowledge or in the area of Christian living if he knows exactly what results he wants before the quarter begins, and if he teaches each lesson during the quarter consciously trying to achieve these specific objectives, than he would if he taught the lessons as they came, wholly unrelated to each other or to any central objective and merely "hope" that some good would come from his teaching. This is so obvious as to need no defense.

It takes time and effort to work out a quarterly aim, but effective teaching cannot be done without it. Teachers must be willing to pay this price or accept responsibility for their ineffectiveness. God helps those who help themselves, but we have no right to expect him to cover up for our unwillingness to give the time and effort to do a really good job of teaching.

We might give the following as an example of a quarterly aim: "My aim this quarter is to help my members to practice three Christian virtues in their daily living: (1) to use the Bible as a guide in making moral decisions, (2) to practice daily communion with God, (3) to engage in personal Christian witnessing." Here, the teacher has three specific objectives in mind that he wants to accomplish. He will thus be able to make each lesson contribute to the achieving of one of these purposes. If the teacher has such a plan in mind at the beginning of the quarter, he has a much better chance of having success at the end of the quarter.

Unit aims.—A unit aim is one which the teacher has for a group of two or more lessons that naturally go together. One lesson period is all too brief a time in which to accomplish a major objective. Thus, as the teacher studies the lessons for the quarter, he will find that there is a group of lessons which are related and which he can use to accomplish the same objective. This becomes a unit aim.

In the aim given as an example above, there would be three unit aims. The aim for Unit One would be to lead the class members to use the Bible as a guide in making moral choices. Let us say that lessons one, two, three, and four deal with this aim. The aim for Unit Two would be to lead the class members to practice daily communion with God. Perhaps lessons five, six, seven, eight, and nine deal with this matter. The aim for Unit Three would be to lead the class members to engage in personal Christian witnessing. Lessons ten, eleven, twelve, and thirteen might deal with this matter. If we were to try to diagram the relation of unit aims to the quarter's aim, it would look as follows:

Aim for quarter

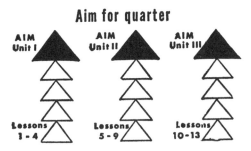

Again, it must be admitted that to work out unit aims may take time and effort but it pays rich dividends in more effective teaching.

Lesson aims.—A lesson aim is one which the teacher works out for each Sunday's lesson. The lesson aim will be discussed more fully in the remainder of the chapter.

Aims and Results

We come now to consider how to determine our aims in order to secure results in Christian living. It has been stated that one of the major reasons we have not had greater results is that our aims have been too vague and too general. One of the qualities of a good aim is that it should be specific enough to be attainable. The question is, just how specific should an aim be?

The objectives of most Sunday school teachers might be subsumed under three major headings: (1) to teach knowledge, (2) to seek inspiration, (3) to secure conduct response.

The practice of most teachers is to try to accomplish all three of these objectives in each lesson. Yet it is a mistake for the teacher to seek to achieve them all in a given lesson. They are not mutually exclusive, but in teaching any given lesson the teacher should have only one of them as the dominant aim. If the teacher wants knowledge, then the knowledge aim will be dominant and will serve as the determining factor in what is taught. If he desires conduct response, then this must become the dominant and directing force in the lesson, determining what is taught and how it is taught. The teacher should have only one of these as his aim, and he must pursue it with undivided effort. Perhaps one of the reasons we have not had more carry-over from classroom teaching into daily life experience is that most of the teaching has been done on an inspirational basis with some general applications or exhortations made at the close of the lesson. Class members may have enjoyed the lesson; they may have had their emotions stirred; they may have agreed with the generalized concepts that the teacher presented—but they *did* nothing about what was taught. The teaching was not sufficiently specific and no definite plans were made in class for this carry-over to take place.

Knowledge, Inspiration, Conduct Response Aims Distinguished

What is meant by a knowledge, inspiration, or conduct response aim? How do they differ? It is a knowledge aim if the dominant purpose of the teacher is to lead the class in a logical, systematic, intensive study of a body of knowledge and to lead to a mastery of that knowledge. An example would be

"To lead my class members to master the essential facts in the Genesis account of creation." It is an inspiration aim if the dominant purpose of the teacher is to lead the class to have a deeper appreciation of some Christian truth or to lead the class to accept or re-accept some generalized ideal. Examples are "To lead my class members to a deeper appreciation of Jesus as the divine Son of God" or To lead my class members to have a deeper social consciousness." It is a conduct response aim if the dominant purpose of the teacher is to lead the individuals to begin to express in a specific way some Christian action in his daily life. This action or response must be observable, and it is preferable if the individual can begin practicing it immediately. It is an observable Christian response in life. An example is "To lead my class to sponsor a recreation program for our young people."

These aims are not mutually exclusive, yet each is distinctive. If a teacher had an inspiration aim, he would obviously use some knowledge and would probably make some application. But the knowledge he would use would not be a logical, systematic, intensive study of a section of biblical content. In an inspiration aim the teacher might use only a very small portion of Bible material or, on the other hand, he may use material from many different sections of the Scriptures. He might also have in mind some conduct response in terms of a generalized application with an exhortation to follow, but there would be no specific plan for a carry-over response.

For example, using the inspiration aim given above, "To lead my class members to develop a deeper social consciousness," the teacher would obviously use some knowledge, but his primary purpose would not be to lead the individual to master a given portion of facts. He would also undoubtedly make some generalized application. The exhortation at the close of the lesson might be "Let's all of us develop a deeper social consciousness." But there would be no definite plans made in class for the members to give expression to a deeper social consciousness in which they would try immediately to eliminate some of the social ills and injustices in their community.

This is not to minimize the importance of developing generalized ideals. They are quite significant. These ideals, attitudes, or convictions give to the individual the goals or purposes for his life, and a person learns in harmony with them. If he has no deep conviction concerning a given problem, little or no learning will take place in that area. One of the major tasks of Christian teaching is to deepen and extend the goals for a person's life in terms of desirable Christian attitudes.

If the teacher has knowledge as an aim, he might have some inspiration and he might arouse a conduct response. However, in a knowledge aim whether he secures inspiration or response is secondary because that is not his real aim. If the members gain a greater mastery of Bible knowledge and a deeper understanding of the meaning of the Scriptures, then the teacher has accomplished his goal for that particular lesson. There are some teachers who say they would never have a purely knowledge aim for any lesson. Is this attitude justified? Is not the mastery of Bible truth an entirely worthy aim? The teacher can set knowledge as his aim for a given lesson, or a given series of lessons, and then have a conduct response for later lessons.

The type of mastery of Bible knowledge being suggested here involves more than the brief Bible passage printed in the lesson quarterly. While this will serve as a guide, the study will certainly not be limited to it. Rather, a knowledge aim should involve a serious study of and, insofar as is possible, a mastery of a relatively sizable and significant portion of the Scriptures. The Uniform Lesson Series often has such a study each quarter. For example, the teacher might decide to make a serious study of the Bible with Bible knowledge as an aim in one of the following areas: The Life of Jesus, The Early Hebrew History, The Period of the Divided Kingdom, The Early Expansion of Christianity.

If the Uniform Lesson Series is used, the teacher, in dealing with the lesson for each Sunday, would obviously have to be concerned with more than the passage of Scripture printed in the quarterly. The lesson would more closely compare with what is referred to as the "larger lesson"; that is, that portion of the Scriptures which serves as the context for the printed passage. Indeed, it would often be necessary for the teacher to go beyond the "larger lesson" because, between last Sunday's lesson and next Sunday's lesson, some Scripture passage which is essential to a systematic and comprehensive study of Bible knowledge may be omitted.

For example, a teacher was leading a class in a serious study of the life of Jesus with a knowledge aim in mind. The lesson for one Sunday dealt with John the Baptist's announcement concerning Christ, recorded in Luke 3. The next Sunday's lesson was about Jesus' preaching in Nazareth, recorded in Luke 4. A look at Robertson's *A Harmony of the Gospels,* revealed that some very significant events had transpired in the life of Jesus between the two mentioned in the lessons above, such as: the naming of the first disciples, the first miracle, the visit to Capernaum, the first cleansing of the Temple, the interview with Nicodemus, and the experience with the woman at the well. If the teacher's aim was to lead the class to have a knowledge of the life of Jesus, he would have to decide whether these experiences should be included in his teaching even though they were not included in the "larger lesson."

The point is, if a teacher has a knowledge aim, he ought so to concentrate on teaching that knowledge that at the end of each lesson and at the end of the quarter his class will have some mastery of it. Such mastery cannot be achieved if the teacher merely "moralizes" about the lesson. This undoubtedly is one reason for the almost unbelievable lack of Bible knowledge on the part of people who attend our Sunday schools. The situation can be remedied if teachers will, at chosen times, concentrate on a strictly knowledge aim rather than try to achieve knowledge, inspiration, and conduct response in the same lesson.

If the teacher has a conduct response aim in mind, he will use some knowledge. Intelligent response must be based upon knowledge. However, the knowledge used will be that which will contribute to the achieving of the desired response and will not be knowledge which comes as a result of a systematic study of a portion of the Bible. In securing conduct response, the teacher also must touch the emotions, or inspire the class, but the aim is not achieved until there is an overt, observable response in the life of the individual.

Perhaps it would help to clarify the distinction between a knowledge aim, an inspiration aim, and a conduct response aim if an example of each were given. First, let us look at the difference in a quarter's aim:

1. Knowledge aim: To lead my class members to learn the significant facts in the life of Jesus in chronological order.

2. Inspiration aim: To lead my class members to have an increasing appreciation of the life and teachings of Jesus.

3. Conduct response: To lead my class members to practice three Christian virtues in their daily experience, to use the Bible as a guide in making moral choices, to practice daily communion with God, and to engage in personal Christian witnessing.

Now let us note the difference as it would be seen in a lesson aim. Let us say that the lesson for next Sunday is on the first missionary journey of Paul and that the teacher has a class of young people:

1. Knowledge aim: To lead my class members to learn the essential facts in the first missionary journey of Paul.

2. Inspiration aim: To lead my class members to be more missionary-minded.

3. Conduct response aim: To lead my class members to engage in a missionary project, such as giving a social for a group of underprivileged children in our city.

The teacher will have a much better chance of securing results in knowledge, inspiration, or conduct response if he will have a clearly-defined aim in only one of these three areas. The teacher's problem arises when he confuses the three and tries to combine them in the same lesson.

Learning to Identify Each Type of Aim

We must learn to identify these different types of aims, for it is the tendency to confuse and combine them that is partially responsible for our failure to secure more concrete and observable results in Christian living. One of the first questions the teacher must answer early in his lesson preparation is this: "Do I want a knowledge, inspiration, or a conduct response aim for this particular lesson?" It may take considerable practice for the teacher to be able to distinguish these three types of aims, but learn he must. If he undertakes to get results in all three areas at the same time, the likelihood is that he will not get satisfactory results in any one of them.

The following questions are given to help the teacher learn to identify the different types of aims:

1. Do I desire this to be a knowledge aim? Is my primary purpose to teach facts, to give information, or to interpret meaning?

2. Do I desire this to be an inspiration aim? Is my primary purpose to deepen appreciation or to develop a general attitude? Knowledge and inspiration aims may be more general than a conduct response aim.

3. Do I desire this to be a conduct response aim? Is my purpose to secure specific response in life? If a conduct response aim is desired, then other questions need to be asked:

(1) Is it brief enough to be remembered?
(2) Is it clear enough to be written down?
(3) Is it specific enough to be attainable? To determine whether the aim is sufficiently specific two further questions must be asked:
a. What do I want the class members to do?
b. How can they express it this week?

Note some examples and apply these tests.

Aim: "To lead my class members to live courageously for Christ." That sounds like a good aim, but actually is it? Let's apply our questions: Is it a knowledge, inspiration, or conduct response aim? (It is a conduct response aim.) Then is it brief? Yes. Is it clear? Yes. Is it specific? No. It is too general. If someone were to ask the teacher what he wanted the class members to do, he would probably reply, "Why I want them to live courageously for Christ, of course." If the person were to persist in asking "But, what specifically do you want your class members to do as an evidence of their courageous Christian living?" it is likely the teacher would find it difficult to think of anything specifically that he wanted his members to do.

That is the problem. A teacher selects an aim that sounds good. In teaching the lesson he leads the group to agree in general that the aim is right (for example, that a Christian ought to live courageously for Christ). But because the teacher has no specific conduct response in mind, the class merely agrees that the teacher is right but leaves the class and makes no specific response. How can the above aim be made more specific? Here is a suggestion: "To lead my class members to say something nice about the handicapped (or colored or foreign) boy when the rest of the crowd is teasing him." This is one way to express courage in living for Christ.

Still another example is "To lead my class members to live a more consecrated life." If this is a conduct response aim, it is far too general. The teacher must ask himself the question, "What do you want the class members to do?" The teacher might reply, "I want them to live the consecrated life." Then the next question must be asked, "How can your class members express this consecrated life this next week?" Thus, the teacher must have in mind some things that the class members are not now doing that they can begin to do and which would enable them to live a more deeply consecrated life. Practically everyone who comes to Sunday school will agree that Christians ought to live a more consecrated life. The difficulty is that so few of us do anything specifically which will help us to live that type of life.

We are beginning to see that one of our major teaching problems in Sunday school is that we have been teaching such vague generalized concepts that everyone who attended Sunday school could agree with them but fail to do anything specifically in carrying out the ideals. For this reason, if we are to get results in Christian living our teaching must become more specific.

VII

WHY AIMS MUST BE SPECIFIC

It was suggested in the preceding chapter that the teacher should not have a knowledge, inspiration, and conduct response aim in the same lesson. The serious teacher considering this approach has asked long before now, "Why can't you have all three aims in a lesson? I don't see how anyone can teach a lesson without having some knowledge, some inspiration, and some conduct response in it." This is readily admitted but does not change our basic contention that, if we are to get results in any one of these areas, one aim must be dominant, and the teacher must seek that one as the primary aim. It is realized that the teacher's past experience is so overwhelmingly on the side of having a generalized aim that when this concept is called into question the teacher will inevitably be exceedingly reluctant to consider any different approach. We are not asking that the reader accept this point of view at this time. We are simply asking that the reader withhold final judgment until after the next four chapters have been read. Only a partial explanation and justification of this approach can be made at this time.

Nevertheless, we want to suggest four reasons why we feel that this approach is valid. In the presentation which follows the emphasis will be on securing results in conduct response. This is being done not because knowledge and inspiration are not entirely worthy and necessary aims, but because the ultimate aim of all Christian teaching is Christian living and because Christianity in action is so desperately needed in our world today.

The Way Character Develops

If teachers are going to secure results in Christian living, the conduct response aim must be dominant and that aim must be very specific because of the way character develops. There is considerable difference of opinion as to how character develops. What is presented here is what seems to the writer to be the best explanation of this complex process. It should be stated that character development is not as simple as pictured here.

In what follows, an emphasis will be placed on securing change in specific areas, but it is recognized that when an individual changes in one specific area, a whole pattern of his experience is changed. Recent findings in psychology suggest to us that the individual responds as a whole to the total situation. Nevertheless, this emphasis on being specific in our teaching is necessary to call attention to the inadequacy of the traditional generalized teaching.

Character grows out of the development of both generalized concepts and specific responses. The individual first accepts a generalized ideal such as honesty, kindness, or unselfishness as the way life ought to be lived. However, while the individual *accepts* the ideal as a whole, the ideal does not automatically operate in all the specific relations of his life. Perhaps the following illustration will clarify this point.

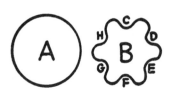

"A" is the generalized concept of honesty which the individual accepts. He believes a person ought to be honest. He has a certain conviction about this matter. "B" indicates those areas of his life (and they may be many) in which he practices this ideal of honesty. But this area does not form a perfect circle as does the general ideal, for few, if any of us, practice a given ideal in all of our relationships. Therefore, "C," "D," "E," "F," and so on, indicate those areas in which he does not practice this ideal. For example, a respectable business-man would never dream of stealing money from a bank, but he might not have any conscience against "stretching things a bit" in making out his income tax returns. Let us change our illustration and use the ideal of kindness. An Interme-diate girl may be exceedingly kind to her pet cat, yet be very unkind to the new girl who has just moved into the neigh-borhood. Or, a six-year-old may be very kind to his school companion but within the hour be grossly unkind to his little sister. Thus we see that, while individuals hold to certain generalized ideals, those ideals usually operate in certain situ-ations and not in others.

It should be stated in passing that it is the function of the inspiration-aim lesson to develop those generalized Christian ideals and convictions out of which specific responses are to come. Inspiration is not to be minimized. It is a matter of basic importance. These ideals must be developed into con-victions that are sufficiently deep to direct decisions and con-trol life.

Why then are generalized inspiration lessons not sufficient for Christian teaching? In the first place, experience has indi-cated that these specific responses do not automatically fol-low the acceptance of a generalized ideal. In the second place, Christian conviction does not automatically give Christian insight to an individual. An individual may desire to be Christian in his family relations but that does not tell him automatically how many times a month he should take his wife out to dinner, nor does it tell him the proper way to discipline his children. Judged by the way that preachers neglect their families, it sometimes seems that they are more unchristian in their home relations than in almost any other area. It may also well be that other men are just as guilty as preachers.

If it is true that it is not sufficient merely to lead an indi-vidual to accept a general Christian ideal, how can these ideals reach out to include those areas in which the person is not now practicing the ideal? Or, rather, how can these specific relationships and situations be brought under the ideal as a controlling and directing factor?

In the class sessions, these specific areas must be lifted to the level of consciousness; that is, the group must be made aware of their failure to express properly the ideal which they hold. The Scriptures are used to throw light on the problem; the members share their ideas, problems, and experiences. The teacher guides the discussion, contributing his insights and experiences. It is in this process that the Holy Spirit has an opportunity to convict each individual of sin (or shortcomings); if this conviction is sufficiently deep, he will change his practice to conform to the ideal. This is conduct response.

It is not sufficient for the teacher to continue to have general aims such as: "To lead my class to be more honest," "To lead my class to be more kind," "To lead my class to be more missionary minded." Rather, the teacher must lift out one specific area in which the class has need, such as: "To lead my class to be more honest in (specific area)." "To lead my class to be more kind in (specific relationship)." "To lead my class to be more missionary minded by (specific response)." If each individual in the class has a different need, adapt the aim to each individual, but be specific for each. For a group of Juniors, an aim might be: "To lead my class to make the home a more happy place by (1) keeping my room straight, (2) hanging up my clothes, (3) making up my bed, (4) mowing the grass, (5) drying the dishes." Each individual in the class could select the specific response he needed most in order to make his home a happier place in which to live.

The point is, teaching in general terms is not adequate for securing conduct response. Rather a person's need lies in those specific areas where he is not now practicing these ideals.

Is there not a danger that this type of teaching might become too personal? Is it not possible that some members will be offended? The key, of course, is the teacher. If he exercises good judgment, if he has good rapport with his class, and if he is a person who in his own life demonstrates that he is seeking to follow that which he is teaching, a large part of the problem will be solved. Then, it should be understood that this type of teaching is based upon a conversion experience in which the individual indicated that his deepest desire was to know and to follow the will of God and the teachings of Jesus. It is an attempt to help the individual discover what the Christian life means in specific situations and specific relationships. If properly conducted by the teacher, there is no reason for a person to be offended. It is simply Christianity in action.

Some may object that these visible results might become mere pharisaical observances. They feel that these conduct responses may be purely mechanical or outward responses in the life of the individual. This danger always confronts experiential and spiritual religion. A spiritual motivation is the only adequate motivation for any Christian action. However, the alternatives are not to have outward expression without spiritual motivation on the one hand or spiritual motivation without outward expression on the other. The ideal is to have Christian action based on spiritual motivation. It is the responsibility of the teacher to keep spiritual motivation dominant in the decisions of his class members.

It should be pointed out that this matter of seeking change on the basis of analyzing specific life situations is not primarily a process of "conditioning" but rather it is a process of developing insight. With his acceptance of a generalized concept as the background or basis, the class member will analyze a specific course of action. With the teacher's guidance, with the Scriptures shedding its light on the problem, and with other members of the class sharing insights and experiences, under the leadership of the Holy Spirit the individual may come to the place where he says to himself, "I see it! I understand it! This is right!" When this insight comes in a specific area, change will take place. This change will not be mechanical but will, instead, be on the basis of conviction of sin and also conviction that a given course of action is right. The spiritual motivation is still basic.

The question might be raised: Does this approach mean that we must deal with every specific response in a person's experience before he can develop a Christian character? The answer is no, but this question brings up the problem of transfer of training. It is possible for those things a person learns in one situation to transfer and influence his response in another situation *under certain conditions.* However, this transfer is not automatic.

There are at least four factors that help to determine whether things learned in one situation will transfer and affect another situation. They are:

1. Whether or not there are common elements in the new situation and the individual's past experiences.

2. The extent to which the individual is aware of these common elements.

3. The depth of conviction he has in this particular area.

4. The strength of other "pulls" in the new situation.

Let's take a situation and see how these factors would affect transfer. We will say that an eight-year-old boy is given a dime to ride the city bus to school. In getting on the bus with a group of children, he forgets to put in his fare. There are so many children getting on at the same time that the bus driver does not notice the omission. Just after he sits down, the boy feels in his pocket and finds the dime. He has been taught the general ideal of honesty. In other experiences, he has been taught that he should not take money from his mother's purse, that he should not pick up apples in the grocery store, that he should not take a pencil from another person's desk at school. What will he do in this new situation? Will his past learning transfer and influence his response in this situation?

The four factors mentioned above do not come in any particular order in a person's experience as he responds to a situation. But, following the order given, are there common elements in the new situation and the individual's past experiences? The experiences that the child has had in the area of forgiveness or in the area of neatness will not affect the new situation he faces because there are no common elements. But he has had certain experiences in the area of honesty, and there are common elements in the new problem he faces and in his past experiences. So there is the possibility that the past experiences in this particular area *may* (not *will*) affect his response.

The second factor is the extent to which the individual is aware of these common elements. As adults, we are able to see them easily, but the child's failure to see that not paying his fare is the same as taking money from a cash register will influence his response. On the other hand, the child might come home after school and say, "Mother, I didn't have to pay my fare today." "Why?" the mother might ask. "Because I forgot to put it in." The mother might then reply with some feeling, "Why son, don't you know that's wrong? That's just the same as stealing." And the child might innocently reply, "Mother, I didn't know it was wrong. I didn't know it was stealing." That is, he saw no connection at all between his failure to give the bus driver his fare and his past experiences in the area of honesty. If this were the case, his past experiences would not affect his response.

A third factor that would influence his response is his depth of conviction in this particular area. If he has developed an intense revulsion toward dishonesty and a deep, inner desire to be honest, his response will be correspondingly influenced. On the other hand, the child may be aware of the common elements; he may know that not paying his fare is wrong. But if he has no strong conviction about honesty or the evils of stealing he may say to himself, "I don't care. I'm going to keep the money anyway." His conviction was not sufficiently strong to influence his response. This is a factor of no little importance, not only on the child level but also on the adult level. There are many who know they ought to do certain things (they ought to go to church, they ought to go to Sunday school, they ought to endeavor to improve a community's welfare, and so on) but they stop there. Their conviction in these particular areas is not very deep, at least not sufficiently deep to call forth corresponding action.

The final factor that might influence the child's response is the other "pulls" that may be in this new situation. Perhaps the child is aware of the common elements and has very strong convictions concerning honesty. But, he may think how nice it would be to use his dime to buy an ice-cream cone after school. It is entirely possible that the desire for the ice-cream cone might outweigh all other factors and be the "pull" which determines his response.

How will the child respond? It will depend on which of these factors are the strongest in his particular situation. A person's acceptance and practice of the ideal of honesty in certain situations does not mean that this learning will transfer automatically and operate in all other situations. Neither does this mean that transfer of training cannot take place. It does mean, first, that we must seek to lead our class members to have as deep convictions as possible and, secondly, that we must deal in specific responses, helping the individuals to see the relation of the particular response to as many other similar responses as possible.

TRANSLATING GENERAL IDEALS INTO SPECIFIC RESPONSES

We have already mentioned the difficulty people have in translating general ideals into specific responses. What does it mean to be thoroughly Christian in our business relations? Surely, to follow the spirit of Jesus in this area of life involves more than just being honest and courteous. However, businessmen often find it difficult to extend this ideal to other specific responses.

Suppose a teacher of twelve-year-old boys was to have as his aim for his next Sunday's lesson "To lead my class to express their love for Jesus in their everyday relationships." Let us apply our tests, given on page 102, to this aim. First, is it a knowledge, inspiration, or conduct response aim? The teacher answers, "I intend for it to be a conduct response aim." Next, is it brief enough to be remembered? We agree that it is. Is it clear? Again, we agree that it is. Is it specific? The teacher replies, "Of course, it is." But, really, is it sufficiently specific? To test whether it is or not we must ask the teacher two more questions: If it is a specific conduct response you are seeking, what do you want your class to do? The teacher replies, "I want them to express their love for Jesus in their daily lives."

Thus the first question is answered; the second question must also be answered. In what specific way do you want the individual to express his love for Jesus? Let me restate this question in terms of a hypothetical situation. Suppose that the teacher has taught his lesson using the above stated aim. After the class, one of the boys comes to the teacher and says in effect, "Mr. Jackson, that was a fine lesson. I want to do as you suggested and try to express my love for Jesus in my daily life. What should I start doing *that I am not now doing* to express this love?" What would the teacher say? There are two possible responses the teacher might make. One is, "I don't know." This would be an unfortunate answer, but some would probably have to make this confession. Another possible response might be, "There are many ways you might express that love." True, but what is one thing that young boy is not now doing that he should start doing immediately? Some teachers will have difficulty thinking of something specific. Then, the teacher can be sure that, more than likely, his class members will not go beyond him in their thinking. Probably, they will simply agree with the teacher's generalized aim and go on living just as they have been. Psychologists tell us that we change our lives in specific areas. We seldom change in general ones. In other words, we do not normally "become good all over."

We are again pointed to the teacher's task to know his

members so intimately that he will know some particular area where they are failing to express their love for Jesus. Then, he may direct the thinking of the class to it, and the members can discuss it openly and frankly. The Holy Spirit will have a chance to work within them in this specific area. If conviction is sufficiently deep, the individual will change his way of living, and the teacher will have brought about a conduct response from his teaching.

This word of caution should be given. The teacher should not expect automatic results because he has a specific conduct response aim. Sometimes, in spite of the best we can do, the individual will make no desirable change. It is the Holy Spirit who is still the great Teacher. But, like the farmer, we must co-operate intelligently with him and provide the conditions which are most favorable for him to do his effective work. We will have a better chance to secure specific conduct response in life when we have a specific conduct response aim in mind than if we have only a general aim in mind.

LIMITED TIME

There is a very practical reason why it is unwise to try to achieve all three types of aims in one lesson. The time we have for teaching is very limited. When the teacher has a knowledge aim in mind, he must seek to stimulate interest on the part of the class in the area to be learned. Motivation that is sufficiently deep to result in action must be aroused. The knowledge to be learned must be presented or discovered. There must follow elaboration, drill, repetition, and review to make the learning last. It takes time to teach knowledge and to teach it well.

The same is true in pursuing an inspiration aim. It takes time to lead people in the study of an ideal or attitude in which their emotions are stirred, their appreciations are heightened, and their convictions are deepened. Certainly, it takes time to secure conduct response. At best, people are reluctant to change. It is not easy to induce people to leave out of their lives certain things which have become habitual or to begin practicing certain Christian virtues which have not been a part of their normal experience.

Thus, thinking in terms of the time factor alone, it becomes obvious that the teacher faces an almost impossible task when he seeks to achieve all three aims in one lesson.

A DIFFERENCE IN APPROACH

Finally, the teacher should use a different approach for each of these types of aims. If he has had as his aim to lead the class to learn the significant facts concerning the first missionary journey of Paul, he would make a quite different approach in his teaching than he would if his aim were to lead his class members to be more missionary minded or to engage in a missionary project. If the teacher has selected a conduct response aim, he will certainly have to use a certain amount of knowledge, but he will not be using the methods of teaching that lead to a mastery of knowledge as such. The approach to be used in securing conduct response is very different from the approach a teacher would use in seeking an inspiration aim or a knowledge aim. The next three chapters will be an elaboration and explanation of this statement.

It should be stated again that, because the emphasis in the following chapters is on conduct response, it is not to be taken as an implication that the other two aims are not entirely worthy. There is a time and a place for each. But, as stated previously, each of them necessitates a different approach. We are presenting the approach that we feel should be used in securing conduct response.

VIII

SECURING PURPOSEFUL BIBLE STUDY

The Bible is the central textbook for teaching religion. The problems and experiences of people can be adequately analyzed and properly directed only in terms of and within the sphere of the Bible. Only within its pages do we come to understand fully the glory and majesty of God and the nature and destiny of man. Unfortunately, Sunday school teachers sometimes use the Bible in such poor and ineffective ways that its impact on the lives of the class members is not nearly what it ought to be.

INEFFECTIVE WAYS TO USE THE BIBLE

This discussion, centering on that portion of the lesson generally referred to as the introduction, is a consideration of principles to follow in stimulating the class and guiding them in their initial consideration of the Scripture passages on which the lesson is based. This is not a study of how the Bible may be used in the development of the lesson.

Most teachers begin on Sunday morning by reading the Scripture suggested for the lesson. But this reading does not usually arouse within the members a sense of holy expectancy and does not elicit from them an enthusiastic response. Why? Probably because the teacher's responsibility to prepare his class for a meaningful Bible study and to arouse within his members a genuine desire to search the Scriptures has not always been completely understood nor adequately accepted. In some classes the Bible is not even used. The teacher and members refer only to the quarterly. At other times, the teacher is the only one in the class who has a Bible. The members never bring their Bibles because they never have occasion to use them.

In still other classes, when the Bible is used, it is not used effectively. Little or no effort is made to stimulate the members' interest in what is being read. The teacher assumes that because the Bible is being read the members automatically will listen. In many adult classes a member of the class is asked to read the Scripture passage, which he does haltingly and without giving meaning to the Scripture. As a result, the class pays no attention to what is being read.

Often, teachers of adolescents will ask each member to read one verse of the Scripture passage. This practice will provide participation, but it is not necessarily a good way to secure purposeful Bible study. Usually, while the first two or three members are reading, the rest of the members are not listening but instead are silently reading the verses they will have to read aloud later. Then, after each person reads his verse, he closes his mind and does not listen to the rest of the group as they read. Again, the Bible is not used effectively.

If an unfamiliar portion of the Scriptures were read in the average Sunday school class, the large majority of the class members would not afterwards be able to tell definitely and specifically what was in the passage after it had been read. Therefore, if we are going to magnify the Bible in our Sunday schools, let us use it in such a way that it will be meaningful and significant.

How to Secure Purposeful Bible Study

How can the teacher secure the attention of the class? How can this attention be deepened into interest? How can he stimulate in the class a desire to open the Bible to see what it has to say about the problem to be studied in the lesson? These are questions the teacher must consider in planning his introduction to the lesson. The Scripture passage should not always be read at the beginning of the lesson, and sometimes may not be read until the middle of the teaching period. At other times, parts of the passage can be read throughout the lesson period. While there is no way to guarantee a serious and meaningful study, the following suggestions should prove helpful.

The class must be prepared for Bible study.—A general rule may be stated here—do not read the Bible as the first thing in the class period. In fact, do not read the Scripture until the class members are ready for it. By being "ready for it" is meant that the teacher has aroused within the class members a desire to want to know what the Scripture passage says. If Bible study is to be purposeful, the group must have a reason for studying it. Their curiosity must be aroused. Their attention must be directed. Therefore, the teacher's task at the beginning of the lesson, by well-chosen questions or statements, is to arouse a deep interest in the members so that they will want to study the particular passage.

The next question naturally follows, how can the members be thus stimulated or how can their interest be aroused? Again, note three simple suggestions:

1. The introduction should be in line with the interest of the group. Whatever the teacher says in his opening statement or statements should appeal to the interest of the members. Obviously, they will not give attention to something in which they are not interested. If the teacher of a class of teen-age boys begins the lesson by talking about Shallum and Menahem, kings of the Northern Kingdom of Israel, he will probably find the boys restless and disinterested. On the other hand, if the teacher begins by referring to the baseball game which the boys saw Saturday afternoon, he will have their attention immediately. The teacher must not assume that because Sunday school is a place for studying the Bible the members will automatically be interested and will give attention.

In determining how to prepare the group for purposeful

Bible study, the teacher should always keep in mind that his purpose in these opening statements is to arouse the members' curiosity. He wants to raise questions in their minds. He wants to stimulate them to do some thinking of their own. One of the best ways to prepare the group is by asking a few carefully planned questions. Or the teacher may accomplish his purpose by beginning with an unusual or striking statement. A good story or illustration may be used. Newspaper clippings or magazine articles and pictures often elicit the interest of the group and may be used effectively.

One teacher of adults, in presenting a lesson on the alcohol problem, cut out a number of lavishly colored advertisements of alcoholic beverages from some magazines. He pasted them end to end and rolled them into a big roll. On Sunday morning, he began the lesson by saying, "I want to show you what I found in some of my magazines last week." Then, holding one end, he threw the roll down the center of the room so that it unrolled before the class. The twenty-foot-long roll of advertisements easily became the center of attention and directed the thought of the group to the Scripture passage to be considered.

Whatever the method of introduction the teacher uses, some vocal response should come from the group before the Bible is read. This expression by the class will help to concentrate their attention and deepen their interest.

2. Keep the introduction in line with the aim of the lesson. It is not enough for the teacher to secure attention by talking about something in which the class might be interested. As was indicated earlier, the teacher of a group of teenagers can always secure their attention by talking about the baseball game or football game that was played Saturday afternoon. But the difficulty is that he may not be able to lead their thinking from the ball game to a consideration of the lesson. Therefore, the teacher's introduction must not only be in line with the interest of the group but with the aim of the lesson, also.

3. Use a natural transition. In the example given above the teacher's possible difficulty in moving into the lesson can be avoided if the transition from the introduction is planned to lead naturally from the discussion of the ball game into a discussion of the lesson. This transition is one of the most important points that the teacher has to consider. Without it, the class may continue in idle talk, discussing any item of interest. The teacher must plan exactly how to direct the group's attention from a consideration of the introduction to the problem to be studied in the lesson.

Tell the group what to look for.—After the teacher has stimulated the interest of the class in line with the purpose of the lesson, he is now ready to take the second step in his effort to secure a purposeful study of the Bible. He tells the group what to look for in the Bible passage before it is read. This will focus the attention on those things the teacher feels are significant for the lesson. It gives the class both purpose and direction in their study.

Many times the writer has read an unfamiliar portion of Scripture to a group of teachers. After the reading he has asked one or two simple questions based on the passage. Overwhelmingly, they have been unable to answer. When the group recognized that they did not know the answers, they always requested, "Read it again." When asked why they wanted it read again the group would reply, "We know what to look for now." Profiting from this experience, the teacher should tell the class in advance what to listen for as the passage is read the first time.

In pointing out to the group what to look for in the Scripture passage to be read, it is usually best to state it in the form of a question. The questions should be limited in number to two or three, for it is not easy to keep more than this number in mind at one time. It may be helpful to have them written on the blackboard. In any case, make sure that the members clearly understand them.

It is not necessary always to ask questions. Sometimes the

teacher may simply say "I would like for you to note the following things as the Scripture passage is read." The teacher
will also think of other variations he might use.

*After the Scripture passage is read ask the class for the
answers to the questions previously asked.*—This is necessary
for at least two reasons: first, in order to make sure that the
class found the right answers to the questions. We often assume that our members know more than they actually do.
Vocal answers to the questions will help the teacher make
sure the members did not get some mistaken idea or will allow him to clear up some confused point. Second, in order
that the class members will understand that the teacher really
means for them to look for the answer. If the teacher asks the
class to find the answer to some question and then never
mentions the matter again, the members soon will ignore
such requests. The asking and answering of these questions
should lead naturally into the discussion or the development
of the lesson.

An Illustration

Perhaps it will help us understand more clearly how to
secure purposeful Bible study if we look at an example. Let
us say a teacher is teaching a class of young adult men. His
aim for the lesson is, "To lead my class members into a deeper
appreciation of Jesus as the divine Son of God." (This is an
inspiration aim.)

TEACHER (at the beginning of the lesson): "Do you know
anyone living today who claims to be God?"

RESPONSE: "Father Divine."

TEACHER: "Does he really claim to be God?"

RESPONSE: "He claims to be."

TEACHER: "To what race of people does he belong?"

RESPONSE: "He is a Negro."

TEACHER: "Since he is a Negro, surely there are no white
people who believe in him, are there?"

RESPONSE: "There surely are. He even has a white wife!"

TEACHER: "Has Father Divine ever performed any miracles?"

RESPONSE: "They claim that he has. They have a lot of crutches they show to visitors."

TEACHER: "What do you think of Father Divine?"

RESPONSE: "I think he is crazy."

RESPONSE: "I think he is a fake."

RESPONSE: "I think he is an impostor."

TEACHER: "What would you have thought of Jesus if you had been living when Jesus was on earth in the flesh?"

For a moment the class sits in silence pondering what their attitude might have been in light of what they have just been saying. Finally, one of the members speaks.

RESPONSE: "I am not sure."

RESPONSE: "I don't know."

TEACHER: "What did the people of Jesus' day think of him? Let us turn to the twelfth chapter of John and find out what their reaction was. As we read verses 12 through 19 and 35 through 43, I would like for you to look for the answers to the following questions:

"1. What was the reaction of the masses of the people?

"2. What was the reaction of the Pharisees?

"3. What was the reaction of some of the chief rulers?"

At this point, everyone in the class opens his Bible, and the teacher or someone else who reads well reads the Scripture.

After the Scripture is read, the teacher asks, "What was the reaction of the masses of the people?" The class responds. The teacher likewise asks the other two questions and then leads naturally into the discussion of the lesson.

AN ANALYSIS

Now let us look at an analysis of the illustration in light of the principles given above. The first principle suggested that the teacher must arouse the interest and curiosity of the class to the point that they have a desire to study the Bible passage.

1. In order to do this, that which the teacher says first must be in line with the interest of the group. The question, "Is anyone living today who claims to be God?" is unusual enough to secure the attention of the group. The questions that follow are designed to deepen their interest and stimulate thought.

2. To secure and deepen the attention of the class into interest is not all that is necessary. There must also be a normal transition from that to the problem to be discussed in the lesson. The transition in the above illustration is the question, "If you had lived at the time when Jesus was on earth— what would you have thought of him?" The class might have been interested in pursuing the discussion of Father Divine further, but this question immediately turned the thinking of the group away from Father Divine and toward Jesus. The transition is so natural that the group almost immediately forgets about Father Divine.

3. That which the teacher uses to secure attention and lead into a purposeful study of the Scripture must also be in line with the aim for the lesson. The question, "What did the people of his day think about him?" is closely related to the lesson.

The second principle suggested was that the class should be told what to look for. There were three questions asked by the teacher. Note that they are also in line with the aim of the lesson. They were: What was the reaction of the masses of the people? What was the reaction of the Pharisees? What was the reaction of some of the chief rulers?

At this point the Scripture passage was read, after which the teacher should ask for the answers to his questions. The asking and answering of the questions lead into the development of the lesson.

Mistakes to Avoid

Having used this plan with teachers for several years, the writer has noted the mistakes that have been made most frequently. To call these errors to the attention of the reader will help him to avoid making them.

First, the plan that the teacher uses to secure interest on the part of the group is in many instances not stimulating enough. The more dramatic one can make this phase of the lesson the better it will be. The ideal or goal of the teacher should be to arouse the curiosity and interest of the group enough to have a genuine desire to open the Bible and see what it has to say. This is not an easy goal, but it is the one toward which the teacher should strive.

Second, too often the teacher fails to plan a normal transition that leads from the interest-getting phase of the introduction to the problem to be considered in the lesson. Because of this failure to have a good transition, the teacher often finds it difficult to lead naturally into the discussion of the lesson. The class continues to talk about the item of interest the teacher has suggested, and the teacher can think of no way to get them off this topic and into the lesson for the day. Thus important time is wasted in idle, useless talk. This transition is important; it must be carefully planned.

Third, in his introduction the teacher may tell the group what is in the Scripture passage rather than leading them to want to know what is in the passage. In so doing they have not been stimulated to a desire to study nor given a purpose for studying the Bible.

Fourth, sometimes the teacher gets too involved in trying to work out a plan to secure purposeful Bible study. Do not let your plan be long, involved, or complex. Be as specific and simple as possible.

Fifth, the teacher often forgets to give the class some questions, the answers to which they are to find as the Scripture passage is read. This is an important part of the whole process. If we are going to lead our class to study the Bible with a purpose, we must tell them specifically what we want them to look for. This will direct their study.

Sixth, the questions must be on the age level of the class

being taught. If the teacher has a group of adults, he would not want to ask them to look for the answers to childish and simple questions that would insult their intelligence. If the teacher has a class of youngsters, he would not want to ask such difficult questions that they would be unable to get the answers. Without being too difficult, the questions should challenge the minds of the class members, whatever their age.

Seventh, sometimes the questions posed are not related to the teacher's aim for the lesson. They should have some relation to it, so that when they are answered the discussion will lead naturally into the development of the lesson.

Eighth, sometimes the teacher tells the group to look for the answers to too many questions. As has been suggested, not over two or three questions should be given to the group.

Let this concluding word be said. A teacher will not always use this method exactly as suggested here. Any plan can get monotonous. However, he will use the same principles involved in this plan. It is the teacher's task to vary the procedure to be followed. But the same principles are used whatever the variation.

Developing the Lesson

Another division of the lesson plan which will be considered only briefly is the development of the lesson. In developing the lesson the teacher should lead the class to a general acceptance of his aim. Thus it is the aim of the lesson that determines what is included in the discussion and what is omitted. What the teacher leaves out is often quite as important as what he leaves in.

Many teachers seem to feel compelled to cover all the material that is given in the lesson helps. If the aim is a specific conduct response, it is not possible to cover all of this material. The teacher should include only that which will contribute to the acceptance of the lesson aim and omit all the rest. The question might be asked, "Why, then, is this material given?" The answer is obvious. One teacher might select a conduct response as his aim, another might select a different aim. Material is given to provide help for as wide a variety of response as possible but should be used only as helps.

Perhaps another even more serious temptation is for the teacher to feel under compulsion to discuss in detail all the verses in the printed Scripture passage. If one has a specific conduct response aim, this also is not possible. Of course, for the knowledge aim and the inspiration aim, the situation is different. For the conduct response, this conclusion is inescapable.

The teacher may ask, "If I have a specific conduct response, will I have to leave out other important truths that are in the Scripture passage?" Yes. The teacher must choose whether he is going to expose his class to a number of important truths or is going to seek a specific conduct response in the lives of his class members. The teacher may ask again, "What am I going to do about those truths which I am forced to omit?" Fortunately, he will have an opportunity to teach the next Sunday and the next and the next. Sometimes in the near future, he will have another opportunity to present the truths that were omitted in a particular lesson.

What is suggested above in no way minimizes the place and importance of the biblical material. Instead, it seeks to magnify Bible study by making it specific. So we come now to say that in the development of the lesson it is the task of the teacher to lead the group in a study of the biblical and theological bases of the Christian attitude under consideration. The attitude being studied or the response being sought must be grounded in a solid biblical and theological orientation which is both understood and accepted by the class. In this way, the teacher seeks to insure that any resulting action or response on the part of the class members will be undertaken from a thoroughly Christian motivation. As Smart says,

Christian ethics divorced from the Christian gospel have no meaning. They are like flowers cut off from their roots. They may live a short time, but they are doomed to die. The Christian standard of conduct is not a natural possibility for any person; it is a supernatural possibility, to be realized only through the redemptive power of Jesus Christ working in human persons through the gospel. Therefore, to impress upon a child, or youth, or adult, his duty to fulfill the Christian standard, and to leave him ignorant of the truth of the gospel which alone makes him aware how that standard is to be fulfilled, is as absurd and exasperating as to order a man to shovel two feet of snow from a hundred feet of sidewalk and give him no shovel with which to do it. Moralism bores us because it confronts us with an impossibility. By the very nature of things, ethics are always insecure until they are firmly rooted in our understanding of truth.[1]

In the development of the lesson, the active participation of the class members should be encouraged. Too often, teachers have considered their task to be to "tell" the members what they (the teachers) had learned from their study or to "tell" what the Bible has to say. This has been a serious weakness in many classes, particularly in adult classes, and to a lesser extent in classes for young people, Intermediates, and even Juniors. Good teaching consists in sharing ideas and experiences by both teacher and members. For this reason the teacher must guard against the temptation to do all of the talking during the class period. There should be an active search for "meaning" as regards the biblical material and a sharing of insights and points of view between teacher and pupils, and pupil and pupil. In and through this the Holy Spirit may have an opportunity to illumine the understanding of each one in the class, including the teacher.

[1] Smart, James D., *The Teaching Ministry of the Church* (Philadelphia: The Westminster Press, 1954), p. 79.

IX

MAKING THE LESSON PERSONAL

Mrs. Hopewell had just finished teaching the Sunday school lesson to her class of Intermediate girls. She was rather pleased with her lesson that morning. The theme was "God's Love for All People." She had brought out the fact that God loves everyone regardless of how rich or how poor they are. She had pointed out that as Christians we should demonstrate the same attitude of love. The girls all seemed to agree that this was the Christian ideal.

On her way into the worship service Mrs. Hopewell passed some of her girls and saw them whispering together, laughing at another girl because of the cheap dress she had on. Her heart sank. The girls had not learned the lesson, after all!

Mrs. Hopewell's problem was the same as that which all Christian teachers face: How to get those whom we teach to apply the teaching to specific situations in their daily lives.

A DIFFICULT TASK

It is not so difficult to cover a portion of Bible material, or to explain a spiritual truth, or even to teach Bible knowledge; but when the teacher tries to instil the spiritual truth into the lives of his class members, he will find that he has undertaken a difficult task.

Two approaches.—To get the spiritual truths of the Bible into the lives of people is the ultimate objective of all Sunday school teaching. In seeking this objective there are two approaches that may be followed.

By and large, Sunday school teachers have followed the

more general approach. That is, the general spiritual truth is presented and explained, the application is made, and the class is exhorted by the teacher to follow the spiritual truth.

For example, during a study of the life of Jesus the teacher may have a lesson on "The Sacrificial Life." In developing the lesson the teacher will perhaps note instances in the life and ministry of Jesus in which he himself had made personal sacrifices, draw some generalized lessons, and then exhort the class to go out and live a sacrificial life.

In the other approach, the teacher must have a more specific aim in mind. He should lead the class to ask themselves the question, "What specifically should I begin doing, that I am not now doing, that would demonstrate my union with Christ in his sacrificial life?" Or, "What should I be doing in the place where I am living which would demonstrate that I have in my life the same missionary spirit that Paul had?" The teacher needs to lead the class to bring out and face specific situations in which they are falling short of the Christian ideal. Only in this way will change in life and action take place.

Reasons why the general approach is inadequate.—A fair and frank analysis of this generalized approach will reveal that it has not been as successful in securing results in Christian living as might be desired. The general approach seems to be based on the assumption that if one knows what is right or if one knows the spiritual truth, he will practice it. Therefore, the teacher conceives his task to be to bring out all the truths in the lesson so that the members will "know" them, with the hope that they will practice them.

However, this assumption is not as valid as we would like to feel—as the story of a man who was selling encyclopedias to farmers illustrates. One day a salesman was putting pressure on a certain farmer, telling how much the set of encyclopedias would help him. He told of all the information in the books that dealt with farming and pointed out how this information could improve the farmer's crops. Without a word, the old farmer listened to the sales talk. Finally he stroked his beard and said, "Now listen son, this set of books you are selling may be able to teach me many things I don't know about farming. But I want to tell you this, I already know a whole lot more about farming than I'm using."

In too many instances those of us who claim to be Christian are like the farmer. While it is true that our knowledge of the Bible is exceedingly limited, on the other hand, it is even more true that we know a lot more about religion than we are using. We know more about soul-winning, forgiving, loving, Christian living than we are practicing.

We must conclude that simply to know a spiritual truth does not necessarily mean that one will follow it. Therefore, we must not rely solely upon a general presentation of spiritual truths to the class members to get desired results.

The mind-set of the class members is often against their making a change in their way of living. While there are many exceptions to this statement, one wonders whether this attitude is not more prevalent than we care to admit. To what extent do people come to Sunday school with the attitude that all that is necessary is to come, to sit, to agree with what is said, and to leave? They all agree in general with the spiritual truth that is presented, but they do not plan to do anything specifically about what is taught and go right on living as they have been living.

Can it be that we teachers and preachers really do not expect our members to do anything definite about what we teach and preach? Are we responsible for our people having developed the attitude that all that is necessary is to come and sit and listen and agree with what is said? If this attitude exists at all, it must be changed before we can get the results in Christian living that we desire.

Unguided Application

It is exceedingly unwise for the teacher to leave the class member to make his own unguided application. Yet, in the final analysis, the member must make his own decision if it is to be meaningful and experiential. "Unguided" is the key word in the above statement. There are teachers who say, "I simply teach the Bible and leave it to my class members to decide what they want to do about it." Such a procedure is not a valid one to follow in securing changes in the lives of people. Let us consider some of the problems involved.

The problem of meaning.—Often the class member may not know the meaning or significance of the teaching of Jesus for his personal life. For example, in the Sermon on the Mount, Jesus says, "Blessed are the poor in spirit." If the class member attempted to carry out this injunction of Jesus, what would he start doing next week, specifically, that he has not been doing? The average class member would find it exceedingly difficult to think of a definite conduct response that would fulfil this teaching of Jesus. (Try to think of one yourself!) As a result, the average member, if left to make his unguided application, would probably make no application at all.

It is not easy to translate the spiritual truths of the Bible into specific conduct responses for daily life. For that reason, the teacher must not wholly rely upon teaching generalized truths. A religious educator tells of an experience a pastor had with some children of his church during a class session. He had talked to them about the Bible verse "Be of good cheer, I have overcome the world." During the discussion the pastor asked the children, "What does this verse of Scripture mean for your personal lives?" The children did not know. He said to them, "It means that in your normal experiences you are to be cheerful in spite of difficulties and hardships." The minister then asked the children to give examples in their daily lives in which this principle could be applied. They could think of none. These children had accepted the teachings of Jesus but, until they received some guidance, did not know how this particular teaching would operate in a specific way in their daily conduct. Some may contend that surely adults ought to be intelligent enough to make applications of Jesus' teachings in their specific life situations, but even for adults it is not so easy.

The problem of relationship.—An individual may not see the relation between a particular life situation in which he finds himself and any spiritual teaching. For example, when a person has suffered a gross injustice at the hands of another, he may not think of the biblical injunction, "Turn the other cheek." Or when an individual comes to vote, he may vote on the basis of party loyalty or prejudice and never think of his spiritual ideals. When he rides through the slum area of his city or through a poor section in the country, he may never think of relating the spiritual teachings which he believes—such as, "Thou shalt love thy neighbor as thyself"—to these social ills. For this reason, he needs guidance in lifting these specific instances to the level of his consciousness. Then the Holy Spirit might convict him for his lack of concern and inactivity in these and other areas. Under that conviction, he may be led to Christian activity and to a higher realm of Christian living.

The problem of prejudice.—Prejudice sometimes makes one unwilling to apply Christian ideals. In the lives of too many of us, prejudice rather than spiritual truth plays the dominant role in determining conduct. When prejudice and spiritual truth come in conflict, people often hold spiritual truths in their minds while their lives are guided by prejudice. Christian people accept the ideal that "God is no respecter of persons." But when this spiritual ideal is made specific with regard to the treatment of minority groups, far too many Christians deny the spiritual truth in practice and are governed by prejudice. People must be led to evaluate their prejudices in specific situations if a change in attitude and conduct is to be secured.

The problem of information.—Often an individual has insufficient information to understand how the Christian ideal would operate in many of the normal relationships of life. He may think he is acting as a Christian when in reality he is merely living up to the current social standard which may be, and probably is, sub-Christian. Consider an individual in his business relations. Perhaps he is not aware that he is unchristian in certain of his activities and relationships because he is not aware that the prevailing business code is unchristian in these areas. Change will not come in his life until these areas are specifically brought to his understanding.

The problem of personal and social pressures.—The individual may be unable or unwilling to make his own specific application because of pressures from society or from within his own life. Being human, we are all subject to the weaknesses of the flesh. In the conflict between the flesh and the Spirit, the individual needs to be helped and guided. For example, when an individual has caught a vision of the high road of the Christian life, there is a deep urge within him to live that high life. But as he looks around him, he sees few who are traveling that road; indeed, most church members are traveling a lower road. Therefore, because of difficulties involved in traveling the higher road and because of weaknesses within himself, he turns from the high road to walk the lower one with the rest of the people. One tragedy of modern Christianity is that we have become so accustomed to traveling this lower road we have identified it as being the norm of Christian living. We are all aware of the weakness of the flesh and the temptation to rationalize our actions to keep from facing the difficulties and the challenge of traveling the higher road.

Take, for example, a man who becomes keenly conscious of some glaring sin in his community. He wants to take his religion seriously and fight that sin. But he knows that if he does, he will "stick out like a sore thumb." People, even church people, will say "He's fanatical" or "He's crazy." No one wants to be considered peculiar, and so the man decides that, since no one else is doing anything about it, he will not either.

Consider a teen-age girl who, like every other teen-age girl, wants "to date." Night after night, she sits by the telephone, waiting for it to ring. She knows what is right and what is wrong. In general, she wants to do what is right. Yet the desire for popularity is so great that she begins to let down her moral standards. People in situations such as these do not need to be left alone to make their own applications. They need to be helped, strengthened, and guided.

The problem of complex situations.—Often there is no clear distinction between right and wrong in many of the complex situations of life. The Christian does not face much difficulty in making decisions when the issues involved are either black or white. But the Christian does have difficulty in making decisions when the issues are gray. There are people who say that if a person really is a Christian he will be able to tell the difference between right and wrong. This is not as simple as it might seem on the surface. For example, a rather large group of preachers were asked the question, "Was it right or was it wrong to drop the atomic bomb on Hiroshima?" About 50 per cent of them said that it was right; the others said it was wrong. The fact that they were Christians did not give them automatic insight into the basic moral in this situation.

Young people particularly are always plaguing their teachers with the question, "Is it wrong to ——?" It is not the task of the teacher to tell individuals dogmatically what is right or wrong. It is his responsibility to lead the group in a thorough, systematic study of the question under consideration that they may determine for themselves what is the Christian attitude or the Christian course of action. After all the facts have been secured, after all the information has been brought to light, after the group has discussed the different viewpoints, in a period of worship the group may be led to decide, each for himself, what is Christian in this particular matter. Of course, it is entirely possible, perhaps probable, that there will continue to be differences of opinion within the group. But, at least, each one in it will come to his own decision on the basis of information and inspiration that he would not have had before such a study was made.

The teacher is not merely a disinterested member of the group while this study is taking place. He is a responsible member of it, making his own contributions for what they may be worth and giving guidance to the whole teaching situation. Naturally, it will be the teacher's desire that the decision will be made with intelligence under the guidance of the Holy Spirit. Because the class members are going to make decisions one way or the other, the teacher must give more attention to helping them solve for themselves the specific problems they face as they seek to discover for themselves what is Christian.

The conclusion seems inescapable that teachers must become more specific in their teaching. Generalized teaching is the basic reason for the teacher's failure to secure more carry-over from his teaching. If we are going to teach for results, we must make the teaching personal. The assumption that the teacher can teach general principles and leave the class members entirely unguided to make their own specific application seems not to be a valid or safe assumption. There are too many things against his making these applications, especially when it would involve change in his life.

By way of analysis, what might happen within the individual who is left to make his own unguided application? First, he may make a valid application and follow it. What has been said thus far is not to be interpreted that Sunday school teaching as it is now being done is a failure. There are those who take the teaching seriously, who earnestly undertake to find and follow the will of God, and who make intelligent application of the teachings. We ought to thank God for these.

The second response is perhaps more prevalent than the first. The individual hears a certain teaching and applies it to the areas in which he is already following it but fails to apply it in other areas. For example, if the lesson is on honesty, an individual may call to mind all of the areas in which he is completely honest, but the probability is that he will not think of the many areas in which he is not honest.

In a third reaction, if the individual does think of some areas in which he is not practicing a certain teaching, the likelihood is that he will rationalize his position to himself and remain of the same mind. Thus the teacher must recognize the fact that it is difficult to secure change. People resist it, particularly when it involves change in attitude or change in personal conduct. Therefore, if teachers are to secure conduct response and action from their teaching, they will have to use something more than generalized teaching and general exhortation to accomplish these desired ends.

How Make the Lesson Personal?

Use a life situation.—The teacher may make the lesson personal through the use of a life situation or, as it may be called, a what-would-you-do situation.

Let us assume that the teacher has already introduced the lesson and secured a purposeful study of the Bible and that he has developed the lesson to the point where there is general acceptance of the aim he has in mind. It is at this point that he plans to use a life situation to make the teaching personal.

Suppose the teacher has a class of ten-year-old boys and has as his aim, "To lead my class members to tell the truth to their parents in spite of difficulties." The following life situation might be used: Jimmy came in from school and found a big piece of chocolate cake on the table. He proceeded to eat it. Later, he heard his mother go in the kitchen and then say in a loud voice, "Who ate that last piece of chocolate cake that I had saved for Mrs. Brown?" Jimmy was scared. Just at that moment his sister, Mary, came in. She had been eating chocolate candy and had chocolate smudges all over her mouth. Naturally, Jimmy's mother thought Mary had eaten the cake. Mary denied it, but her mother would not believe her. The mother said, "Mary, I know you ate that piece of cake and I am going to punish you for doing it." Jimmy was quiet, but he was thinking hard. He knew if he kept quiet Mary would get the punishment. What would you do?

In leading the class to face this situation, the teacher would be leading them to consider the lesson aim of telling the truth to parents in spite of difficulties. This type of situation would also make the lesson real to the class. Earlier in the lesson the group may have agreed that all boys and girls ought to tell the truth to their parents. But when they are confronted with a life situation such as this, they will no longer answer glibly or consider the matter superficially. In a life situation, they see what the teacher is talking about and realize that they themselves might be involved in a similar situation.

Or perhaps the teacher has a class of young people. Having the same aim, he might use this life situation: Tom is a senior in high school and has been driving the car by himself for about a year. One day Tom's dad called him in and said, "Tom, you know that you and I have always shot straight with one another. You also know that I have never tried to spy on you in order to catch you doing something. However, word has come to me that you have been driving the car rather fast and recklessly. Son, we want to have an understanding. I am going to trust you to drive the car properly. I am not going to be a watch-dog to see whether you do or not. I am going to trust you. However, if you ever get a traffic ticket for speeding, I will take away your privilege of using the car for three months. Is that fair, son?"

Tom admitted that he had been driving the car too fast sometimes and he agreed that what his dad proposed was fair and was perfectly satisfactory with him.

Some months passed. Tom had forgotten the conversation with his father. One night he and Jerry were double-dating with their best girl friends. They were having a wonderful time talking over plans for winning the prize at the scavenger hunt to be held soon. They were so excited with their plans that Tom forgot to watch the speedometer. Before long, a siren was heard behind them. A police officer handed Tom a ticket for speeding. It was then that he recalled with a shock his conversation with his father. With downcast face Tom told his friends about it and said he would not be able to use the car for the scavenger hunt as they had planned. The group was keenly disappointed. Then Jerry said, "Tom, I have an idea. You give me the traffic ticket and I'll pay it for you. Your dad need never know anything about it." The girls joyously agreed that this was the right solution. Tom hesitated. What would you do?

When this life situation was used in teaching a group of young men, one of them said, "I would wait until after the scavenger hunt and then tell Dad about it." His solution was an indication that he had failed to see the full implications of telling the truth. Real truthfulness for the Christian is a willingness to tell the truth regardless of the consequences, even though the individual knows that punishment will follow. Although the young man's response was an indication that the lesson had become realistic for him, it also indicated that the truth, though accepted, had not been fully learned.

Principles involved.—What are the principles to be followed in working out a life situation? First, it must be a realistic life situation. The term "life situation" in the sense in which it is used here does not mean that it must be a true life experience. It simply means that it is a situation, real or imaginary, which is related to the normal experiences of the class members. It should be a situation in which there is drama, action, and suspense, one in which a decision must be made.

The important thing is that it must have the ring of realism for the class. For example, if the teacher had an average group of children, he would not use a situation in which the individual involved had to determine what to do with a million dollars. Such a situation would not be real for this group.

He might use a situation in which a decision had to be made concerning what to do with fifty cents. The teacher should take care to work out a situation in which the members could easily be involved. It should be so realistic that the class would identify themselves with it and become emotionally involved in it. To achieve this, it must be related to their normal experiences.

Second, it must be a situation in which two courses of action are presented. One is the "human" one. In following this course of action, the individual would be "doing what comes naturally." For example, in the first life situation given earlier in this chapter, the "natural" thing for Jimmy to do would be to remain quiet and let his little sister get the punishment. In the second life situation, the "natural" course of action would be for Tommy not to tell his dad he had gotten the traffic ticket. In working up a life situation, it is important that the teacher put into it all of the pulls and tugs he can to make the "human" course of action the more desirable one to follow. That is the way life does. The Christian course of action is the other alternative. Of course, in presenting the life situation, the teacher does not say that there are two ways open for the group to follow. But he takes care to see that the two possible courses of action are involved.

In the third place, the life situation must be one in which the class will apply the teacher's lesson aim in making the proper choice. In the example of Jimmy and the cake, if he had chosen to confess that he had eaten the cake even though he knew his mother would have punished him, then he would have been fulfilling the aim of the lesson which was "to tell the truth in spite of difficulty." The teacher does not reveal the lesson aim to the class, but it must be inherent in the situation.

Using a "life situation" is not the same as "applying the lesson" to life. The objective is the same, but the approach is different. In the latter the teacher undertakes to point out, usually in general terms, how the truths that have been discussed in the lesson would apply to life. He concludes with an exhortation to the class to follow them. A life situation makes no generalized application but presents the spiritual problem involved in the lesson in terms of a realistic, specific situation in which the members could easily be involved. It takes the spiritual truth out of the realm of the abstract or theoretical. This approach enables all age groups to see much more clearly the relation of a religious truth to life because it is presented in terms of a concrete life situation. A conflict is involved; a choice must be made.

A life situation is not the same thing as an illustration. An illustration is a story or incident that is complete in itself. In an illustration the end or outcome is told. In a life situation the end or outcome is not told. The group is led to the point at which a decision must be made, but the decision is not given. At the climax of the conflict, when the struggle between the human and the Christian response is at its peak, the teacher confronts the members with the question, "What would you do?" This is one of the values of a life situation: Since the outcome is not told, the way is opened for discussion of possible outcomes that may be suggested by the members of the class.

A life situation does not have to be a true story. It may simply be a hypothetical situation that comes from the imagination of the teacher. However, the teacher must know the members of the class so well that he will be able to make up situations so closely related to the normal experiences of the group that they are real to them; otherwise they will be of little or no value.

If the class members do not respond when the teacher asks "What would you do?" the teacher must lead the group to confront the issue until they do. He should give the class some time to think and then ask, "Well, what *would* you do?" It may be that they are not sure what they would do. It may be that for the first time they are beginning to see how the spiritual truth can be operative in their daily experiences.

What should be done if the class members respond lightly? What if one of the members of the group gives the "correct" answer just because he knows it is the "correct" answer? The teacher will have to discern whether the answer is sincere. If the answer is given lightly, there are at least two things that the teacher might do. He might ask, "Is that what you *really* would do?" A few probing questions such as this will let the class members know that he will not be satisfied with any light answer. Or, if the situation is so real that the class has become emotionally involved, the other members will usually take down the one who answered lightly with the proverbial "Oh yeah!" Often the other members of the class can handle such a situation more effectively than the teacher can.

It is important that the teacher save ample time for this part of the lesson. If the problem is real to the group and the decision is difficult to make, it is likely that the teacher will have to lead the group in re-thinking the spiritual truth which had been so glibly accepted before. As the group discusses the difficulties involved and the courses of action possible, they may be telling the teacher what they really think for the first time instead of what they think the teacher wants them to think. After seeing what the spiritual truth might mean in a specific life situation, it may be necessary for the teacher to begin again and to lead the class to re-accept the aim he has in mind.

Using a life situation is only one more or less dramatic way to make the lesson personal. There are other more simple ways. For example, the teacher might say, "What does this lesson mean for your personal lives?" Or, the teacher might say to the class, "You give me a situation from your experience in which this spiritual truth we have been considering would be involved." Here, as in all teaching, variety is the spice of life. Certainly, the teacher will not use a life situation every Sunday. Probably it should not be used over once a month. It will be up to the teacher to devise other ways of making the lesson personal so that the class members will be led to see the relationship of the spiritual truth to their personal lives.

MISTAKES TO AVOID

There are some common mistakes made in using life situations. Many times the life situation lacks "punch" or climax. It must have such fascination and appeal that the group is drawn so strongly into the situation they identify themselves with the characters in the situation.

To use the second person rather than the third person in the situation weakens it. It is better for the members of the class to be left outside of the situation. Then they can look at it objectively until they are brought into it with the question, "What would you do?"

When the life situation is not sufficiently related to the aim of the lesson there is a lack of unity. If the teacher's aim has to do with some phase of reverence, it would be of no value to have a life situation dealing with neatness. The teacher's aim must determine everything that goes into the lesson. The Bible study, the development of the lesson, the life situation, all must be related to it.

Teachers often use illustrations and think they are life situations. As noted earlier, they are not the same. An illustration tells a story; a life situation presents alternatives. It should also be pointed out that the life situation is weakened when the teacher suggests alternatives to the class. For example, after telling a life situation the teacher should not say, "Would you do this or would you do that?" It is better to omit the alternatives and leave the decision completely open without suggesting any possible course of action. The class may present some alternatives that the teacher has not considered, and to suggest some limits the thinking of the class.

Sometimes the "right" answer to the alternatives that are presented is too obvious. The decision is too easy. When this is the case, it is usually because the teacher has not put into the situation all the temptations and attractions, pulls and passions, that are in real life situations and that lead the individual to make the "human" choice. At other times, the situation is not sufficiently real to the group. These situations, if they are to be real, must center in the main-line interests of the group. The teacher should ask himself the question, "Could this happen, or is this situation likely to happen, to any of the members of my class?"

Finally, in some instances the situation is not sufficiently related to the age group. If a teacher has a group of Juniors, he would not use a situation suitable to a group of college students.

It is not easy for a teacher to make his teaching personal. But unless he does, the teachings of Jesus will not become the living and guiding force in daily life that they ought to be. The results are worthy of whatever efforts the teacher may have to expend.

X

SECURING CARRY-OVER

We have said that one of the problems we confront in teaching in the Sunday school is that the lesson does not sufficiently carry over into the lives of the class members. Probably one reason for this is that the teacher does not make specific plans for a carry-over to take place. In concluding the lesson, the teacher often makes some general application of it and exhorts the class to comply. Or, in some instances, the bell rings before the lesson is finished, and the teacher is forced to make some hurried, concluding comments before the class is dismissed. If the teacher expects to secure definite results from his teaching, something more than this is needed.

PLAN FOR CARRY-OVER

Teachers often fail to secure results because no plans were made for results to be obtained. Too often, the teacher leaves the results "up in the air." The time to remedy this is when the lesson is being prepared. Securing carry-over should be as definite a part of the lesson plan as the development of the lesson or making the lesson personal.

Carry-over involves two things: first, a decision by the class concerning what can and should be done; second, a plan for definite action. It may be either individual or group action, depending on the nature of the project. A class of Juniors may decide to start reading their Bibles daily; this would involve individual action. A class of young adults may decide to sponsor a recreation program for the young people in the church; this would involve group action. The response will take place outside the classroom, but the decision for action and at least the initial plan for action must take place within the classroom.

In the teacher's lesson plan, there should be a section headed "How to Secure Carry-over." When the teacher determines what specific conduct response he would like the class members to make as the result of the teaching of this lesson, he also plans how he will lead the group to choose this response as their own.

The response decided upon by the class should be acted upon immediately. Of course, there will be times when it is impossible for the group to react to a spiritual truth that quickly. Months or even years may pass before the full fruit of the teaching may be seen. But teachers have leaned too heavily upon this concept and too often have used it as an excuse for poor and ineffective teaching. The teacher should try to make his teaching and the response so specific that the class members will be able to begin demonstrating an evidence of the spiritual truth in their lives during the following week.

MEMBERS MAKE THEIR OWN SUGGESTIONS

While the teacher must make definite plans for this carry-over, it is far better for the class members to make their own suggestions as to what they can and will do the following week. How may a teacher accomplish this result? It must be remembered that action imposed by an outside authority (such as the teacher) probably will not be meaningful in the experience of the group. For the decision or course of action to be meaningful to the individual, the individual must choose it for himself. This is eminently true in the realm of moral attitudes or spiritual action.

Three things should be kept in mind: In the first place, while the teacher may make plans for a certain response by class members, it is entirely possible for the members of the class to choose a different response. If the response chosen by the class is worthy and Christian, it is entirely acceptable. In fact, it will be better than the one the teacher had in mind because it is their idea. Of course, the teacher might have several possible responses in mind, and each individual in the class could come to a different response in light of his own particular need and interest. Such decisions would be both legitimate and worthy, for the teacher would not have imposed his idea upon the class, and their responses would be individually chosen.

In the second place, even though the teacher makes the suggestion as to a possible response, it is possible for the class to select this response for themselves. A father may come home on a hot summer afternoon and say to his two boys, "Let's go swimming." If the boys reply enthusiastically, "Oh, boy! Let's do!" he has not imposed his will on the boys. Their response is just as surely self-chosen as if the boys had made the suggestion themselves.

In the third place, it is important that the response have meaning for the learner. For that to occur, the learner must have insight into both the situation he confronts and the desired response in that situation. He must clearly see the issues involved in a given response. He must be made aware of the conflicting interests, desires, and passions within his own life. Jesus constantly sought to lead his followers to understand what following him involved. "If any man would come after me," he said, adding in effect, let him count the cost.

The learner must not respond on a superficial basis such as to please a teacher. He must be led to face the situation frankly and, in the light of the total commitment of his life to Jesus and of his accepted generalized ideals in this particular situation, to choose what to him seems to be the Christian response. There must be true individual choice with no external pressure exerted. The decision must come from deep within the learner if it is to be either Christian or lasting.

FOLLOW-UP BY THE TEACHER

The teacher needs some plan to find out whether the lives of the members are really being influenced by his teaching. Admittedly, this is difficult to do. But in too many instances teachers have no idea whether or not their teaching is making any significant difference in the lives of their class members. They have only the vague hope that they are "doing some good." If the teacher is to expect results, if he is to obtain results, this vague hope is not sufficient. He must find out what is actually happening in the lives of those whom he teaches.

There are several different plans the teacher may use in securing this information. With pre-adolescent children he might simply ask for a report on what they did during the week to carry out the decisions made in class the previous Sunday. If the class decided on a group project, the teacher may observe them at work. With the younger age-groups the teacher may have personal conferences with parents or, in parent-teacher meetings, discuss the actions or behavior of the child in the areas in which the teacher has sought conduct response. In certain instances the teacher will be able to sense much of this information through individual, informal talks with the class members.

A plan for follow-up is needed to let the class members know that the teacher really expects them to do something about what is taught on Sunday morning. Some class members have gotten into such a habit of agreeing with what the teacher says without making any definite response to the teaching that they do not realize the teacher really expects them to do something about it. The understanding must be instilled in the minds of the class members that this teaching is for life and for action.

The check-up plan will vary according to the age group. It will be most difficult with a group of adults and easiest with Intermediates, Juniors, and younger children. But regardless of how difficult it may be, if results are to be achieved, a follow-up must be made. This is not to suggest that the teacher be a spy who tries to catch his members when they do not respond properly. It simply means that an interested teacher is vitally concerned whether or not his members are growing as Christians. It means he is not willing to leave his teaching to chance.

An Example

An example might help the reader to understand more clearly how a teacher might go about trying to secure this carry-over. Let us say the teacher is dealing with a class of twelve-year-old boys. He has as his aim, "To lead my class members to be regular in attendance at the morning preaching service for the next quarter." He has led the group in a meaningful study of the Bible and to accept in general the idea that Christian people should worship God regularly. After this, he presents the class with a life situation in which they see something of the difficulty involved in regular church attendance. After further study and discussion, the group accepts the aim that people should worship God regularly in spite of difficulties. The teacher then comes to the carry-over.

TEACHER: "Do any of you know what percentage of our class attended church regularly last quarter?"

RESPONSE: "No."

TEACHER (writing on the blackboard): "We had only 45 per cent."

RESPONSE: "That's not good."

TEACHER: "No, that isn't good. In light of our discussion today what do you think our class percentage for church attendance ought to be next quarter?"

RESPONSE: "It ought to be 100 per cent."

TEACHER: "Certainly, that is the ideal. But let us be more realistic. What per cent do you think we actually ought to try to reach for this next quarter?"

RESPONSE: "Eighty-five per cent."

RESPONSE: "Sixty per cent."

RESPONSE: "Seventy-five per cent."

TEACHER: "I see we have different ideas concerning the matter."

After discussion, the class agrees on a certain percentage.

TEACHER: "Now what are we going to do to help ourselves reach this percentage? We haven't reached it in the past, so if we are going to reach it, we will have to do more work than we have been doing. Does anyone have any suggestions that will help us reach this goal?"

RESPONSE: "Let's all sit together at the preaching service this next quarter."

THE REST OF THE CLASS: "Yes. That would be great!"

TEACHER: "All right, I will contact your parents and ask them if that will be agreeable with them. Is there any other suggestion you may have?"

RESPONSE: "We might have a committee to telephone everybody in the class on Saturday and remind them to stay for church on Sunday."

TEACHER: "That is a good suggestion. Who would you like to have on that committee?"

RESPONSE: "I think it is too much to ask one committee to call the members of the class for three whole months. Would it not be better to have three committees and let them phone for only one month each?"

TEACHER: "That is an excellent idea. Then let's select three committees."

The discussion continues until definite and specific plans are made to secure the carry-over in the lives of the class members.

A group of adults might have a lesson on Christian growth. A conduct response aim might be, "To lead each member to engage in a serious, systematic study of the Bible for this quarter." In the traditional approach to this lesson, the teacher would call attention to the fact that one way to grow is through studying the Bible. He would then conclude the lesson with the exhortation, "Let's all study the Bible more." The class would agree but it is likely that the members would make no specific response.

In the approach being suggested here, the teacher would seek to lead the group to make definite plans for carry-over to take place. In developing the lesson and in making the lesson personal, the teacher would lead the group to a commitment to the idea that we need to study the Scriptures more intensively. In the carry-over, the teacher would call attention to the fact that usually a general commitment to Bible study is not sufficient because the press of daily affairs soon crowds it out. He would suggest to the group that they consider setting up a systematic schedule for daily study for one quarter. Various schedules and the problems involved would be considered. What portion of the Bible might be used in this study would also be considered.

The teacher would lead the class to consider what aids they might want to use to make their study of the Bible more understandable and meaningful. Too often the average person becomes discouraged in his study of the Bible because he does not understand what he reads. If the group decides they would like to study the Gospel of John as their project for the next three months, the teacher should have brought from the church library an inexpensive commentary on the New Testament. He should indicate the help it would be to them as an aid in Bible study. Questions would be asked and answered, problems would be raised, and the discussion would continue until specific plans were made for the carry-over to take place.

This is the key to the success of the lesson.—This is the point at which the nail is driven up to the head. All of the rest of the lesson has been generalized discussion about what might or should be done. In this portion of the lesson, each member is led to consider *what he is going to do.* Therefore, because this part of the lesson is so important it is necessary for the teacher to save plenty of time. If the bell ends the class session before the conclusion is reached, it is likely the values of the entire lesson will be lost. This conclusion must be unhurried. It takes time for the class members to think, to make decisions, to draw conclusions, and to make specific plans as to what they will do.

It may be that this matter of carry-over is the most important and least used of the entire lesson plan. Many teachers may have a specific objective. They may start with the interest of the group and lead to a purposeful study of the Bible. They may have an interesting development of the lesson and then make a very practical application of it. But at this point they stop short and fail to secure the carry-over into life experience.

The teacher makes the application and then exhorts the class to practice it in a fashion similar to this: "Christ helped those in need; let us follow his example." Or, "Jesus is our example. Let's try to follow his example." Or, "We are living in a sinful world. Let's try to make our world a better place in which to live." Then the class is dismissed with prayer and no specific plans are made through which the members may carry out the matter discussed in the lesson. As a result, the likelihood is that the members, having agreed with the generalized concept, will go out and do nothing.

In certain instances, the course of action decided on by the class will be too involved for plans to be worked out fully in the class period. In this case, it may be that the class will want to have a special meeting during the week to work out the details of the plan to be followed. Or, the class may appoint a committee to study the problems and report to the class the following Sunday.

A teacher of an adult class had as his aim, "To lead my class to take some positive steps to provide a more wholesome environment for the social life of our high school group." In teaching the lesson he pointed out some of the evils in the community which served as a source of temptation to young people. One of the class members replied that something ought to be done to eliminate these evils and to provide a more positively Christian environment for the high school students. The teacher faced the class with the suggestion, and the class unanimously decided to undertake this as a class project.

This project was, of course, too involved to be worked out in the class period. The class decided to meet at the teacher's home on Tuesday night for discussion and planning. At this meeting, they considered such questions as: What shall be our plan of attack on this problem? What facilities of a Christian nature are available to our young people? What facilities of a questionable nature are available to our young people? What facilities of a distinctly unchristian nature are available to our young people? Shall we make a survey as to where and how our young people spend their leisure time? What committees do we need? Questions were faced. Answers were sought. Other meetings were held. The course of action was decided upon and put into effect.

Planning sessions such as these will not simply end in "talk" or with a general exhortation—"Let's all try to help our young people"—but in action. It could well be that in carrying out a project of this type, the class members might learn more practical Christianity than they would learn from just listening to a teacher for a number of Sundays.

ADVANTAGES OF GROUP DECISION

Although a study of the principles and factors involved in group dynamics is a rewarding experience, if undertaken seriously, it is not our purpose here to go into this rather specialized area.[1] We simply want to point out some advantages that group discussion, group decision, and group action have over the practice of leaving the individual to make his decision alone.

[1] For those who are interested in the study of group dynamics we suggest the following as good, popular treatments of the subject: Wittenberg, Rudolph M., *The Art of Group Discipline* (New York: Association Press, 1951); *So You Want to Help People* (New York: Association Press, 1947).

Some objections met.—There are teachers who say, "I just teach the spiritual truth and let the class members make their own application because I don't know what their particular needs are." Such an admission on the part of the teacher is no justification for ineffective teaching nor does it invalidate the principle that is here being suggested. It is the responsibility of the teacher to know the individual class members well enough to know what their particular needs are.

Other teachers say, "I teach the general truth because my class members need different things. When I teach the truth in general terms, each member is left free to make his own application." It is true that the class members will have needs that differ, but this simply indicates that it is the teacher's responsibility to adapt the spiritual teaching according to the differing needs of each individual.

Another teacher may say, "I don't want to be too personal." This is a valid consideration on the part of the teacher that must be faced. When a teacher leads the group to analyze and evaluate their present experience in light of some spiritual ideal, the discussion undoubtedly is getting personal. The teacher may feel that this kind of teaching is too personal and that the class members will resent it.

Three things need to be said. First, it would depend upon the attitude and spirit of the teacher as to whether the class members would object to this kind of teaching. If the teacher has built up the proper relationship between himself and his class members, if he demonstrates a sympathetic attitude toward the problems and viewpoints of all the class members, and if the class members understand and appreciate the approach of the teacher, they will welcome rather than resent such teaching.

In the second place, he must use common sense in this type of teaching. He must recognize where his members are in relation to a given Christian attitude and lead them step by step toward the ideal. He should not try to lead them to take too long a step at any one time. Insofar as is possible, the teacher should deal with problems objectively rather than subjectively and personally.

In the third place, it must be admitted that there are probably some individuals who would resent having Sunday school teaching become this personal. They would rather come to a class where the Bible truth is taught and their lives are not bothered. There are people who will accept everything that Christianity teaches so long as it does not affect or change their way of living. But when Christianity makes demands that would necessitate changes, they get their feelings hurt and stop coming to church. In answering this objection, the teacher must decide for himself whether his task is to rock people to sleep or to seek to lead them to grow in the likeness of Christ.

A positive view.—As a general rule people are more willing to make a change as a member of a group rather than as an individual. When an individual is left alone to make his own decision, he misses the benefit of the thinking of the group. He does not know about the victories that have been won by other members of the class in the particular area that is being considered. He does not know of the struggles and difficulties that others have faced and overcome with regard to a given course of action. As a result of missing all of this, he feels that he is the only one who faces this problem, and he tends to rationalize his position and continue in his present attitude.

On the other hand, as a member of the group he has the benefit of group thinking and group discussion. He hears and evaluates the ideas and points of view of others. In hearing of their problems, their struggles, their victories, the individual is strengthened and encouraged to do what he knows he ought to do.

In the second place, to follow a given course of action as a member of a group becomes an adventure and a challenge. A class of young adults may decide to do something about the "joint" that is on the corner two blocks from the church. One man alone would not think of doing anything about it, but the same individual, as a member of a group, would consider this course of action a real challenge to his Christianity.

As a member of a group the individual has group support. If, with the group, he engages in a course of action that is unusual; if for example, he undertakes to fight some flagrant sin in the community, he does not feel that he is being fanatical. He is not the only one "sticking his neck out" when he works with a group. He is willing to do things as a member of the group that he would never have the courage to do alone.

There is no guarantee that if a teacher will follow this plan carry-over will take place. It is simply that a teacher, using this plan, will have a better chance to secure carry-over in the lives of class members than he would if he followed the plan of making a general application.

XI

A LESSON PLAN

How will the teacher prepare the lesson he is to present to his class next Sunday? What plan will he use? There are as many different ways of planning a lesson as there are teachers, and no one plan is "best." Two teachers may use two completely different plans, and both of them may be excellent. Lesson plans will also vary with different age groups. The small children may be taught through centers of interest. Older children may have an "early time" or "pre-class" session. Teachers need to have a lesson plan adaptable to their particular age-group's need. However, the principles underlying the plan that is suggested here will still be applicable.

It is feared that many teachers follow a rather haphazard approach in their lesson preparation. Some feel that they can wait until Saturday night to begin their lesson preparation. They scan the material given in the denominational lesson helps, read the suggested Scripture passage, get the general idea of the lesson, and then try to teach from this type of slipshod preparation. It is no wonder we have obtained so little results from our teaching. If teachers are serious in their desire to lead their class members to grow in the likeness of Christ, to express in their normal everyday experiences the ideals of the Christian faith, this type of haphazard, incidental, and unworthy approach to lesson preparation will have to cease. Effective teaching demands the most careful preparation.

PRACTICAL AIDS IN LESSON PREPARATION

It is helpful to consider some introductory matters before giving our attention to a suggested lesson plan.

Have a definite time for study.—The study of next Sunday's lesson ought to begin early in the week. Some begin on Sunday afternoon, but certainly every teacher should begin preparation by Monday if he is to meet the particular needs of his class and make the lesson real, personal, and alive for them. To find an introduction to the lesson that will immediately capture the attention of the class, or to find the right illustration to drive home a point, or to work out a life situation to make the lesson personal for the group requires a lot of time.

Not only should the study begin early, but definite times should be allotted during the rest of the week for the teacher to continue his study. Unless definite periods are set aside the teacher will find that other matters interfere and his time for study will be pushed aside. Once time has been set, it should be kept as faithfully as would an engagement with an important person. It should be a time when there is a minimum of noise and interruption, perhaps when the children have gone to school or to bed. Whenever it is, it should be a time of meditation and concentrated study.

Have a definite place for study.—Many teachers have found it advantageous to have a definite place for study. If a teacher has a place where he is quiet and alone, the place will develop an atmosphere that is conducive to meditation, prayer, and study. Another advantage to such an arrangement is the possibility of having all needed materials readily available. It is exasperating to be ready to study and then have to spend time trying to find the lesson quarterly. To remedy this, the teacher can keep his Bible, his lesson helps, his commentaries, and other materials all in one place so they will be available when needed.

Materials needed for study.—The study materials necessary will be partially determined by how much the teacher can afford to purchase. As a minimum, two good Bibles—one of them a good modern translation—and the lesson helps supplied by the denomination. In addition to these, he will find the following helpful: *Broadman Comments, Rozell's Complete Lessons, Peloubet's Select Notes, The Douglass Sunday School Lessons, Tarbell's Teacher's Guide.* He should also have a good one-volume commentary of the Bible, a Bible dictionary, a Bible atlas, and a concordance. (See materials suggested at end of chapter.) He should also have at his fingertips a notebook having information about and, if possible, pictures of his class members. As the lesson is being prepared, he will refer frequently to this notebook to discover the different interests of the class members as well as their different needs. To have this intimate knowledge of the members of the class is an absolute essential.

The teacher's preparation of himself.—As the teacher begins his preparation, it is readily apparent that his own attitude is quite important. Since he cannot do his best when he is tired, worried, or distraught, he should, if possible, plan his study when he is rested. If the cares and worries of the day weigh heavily upon him, he may prepare his own heart by a few minutes of meditation and prayer.

Physical preparation is not all. In studying the lesson the teacher must ask himself questions such as these: What does this particular lesson mean to me? Have I had any experiences with Christ in this area? Do I have the kind of faith I am going to try to teach next Sunday? Have I had experiences in prayer sufficient to teach my class? Do I have the missionary zeal that I need? Am I the kind of Christian witness I should be? Basically, teaching is a sharing of experiences, and the teacher cannot share that which he himself has not experienced. Class members of every age sense any sham and pretense. So the teacher must prepare his own life if he would teach effectively.

THE TEACHER PLANS THE LESSON

When the teacher is ready to begin specific preparation for next Sunday's lesson, he should, first of all, read the entire Scripture passage that is suggested in the "larger lesson." After he gets, in this way, the general background out of which the lesson was selected, he is ready for more intensive study. He will want to read the passage in a good modern translation. This should be followed by a careful study of the interpretation and comments in a reliable commentary. Any unfamiliar names or places should be looked up in a Bible dictionary. Everything possible should be done to master both the content and the interpretation of the suggested Scripture passage. Then he should consider carefully the suggestions given in the denominational lesson helps and any other helps he has available.

After familiarizing himself with the truths in the Scripture, he is ready to turn to the notebook containing information about his class members. As he scans the information concerning each member, he asks himself what each one needs most from this lesson. In light of the answers to this question he selects a lesson aim and is ready to devise his plan for securing the attention and interest of the class and leading them in a purposeful study of the Bible.

Next comes the problem of developing the lesson. There are two things the teacher must keep in mind particularly. First, he must remember that in this part of the lesson he wants his class to accept the general ideal that underlies his aim for the lesson. To accomplish this he must include all the material time will allow to lead his members to this acceptance and must leave out of the lesson all those truths which are as interesting and as important but which do not contribute specifically to the acceptance of his aim.

Second, he must keep in mind that the lesson development must be designed to meet the need of each individual in the class. Because each member is different, the need of each will be different. A question may have to be asked especially for Mary's benefit. An illustration may have to be told in order to meet Ellen's need. A problem may need to be discussed for Joan to see her particular problem. The question is, does the teacher know the members of the class intimately enough to know what their particular needs are?

Lastly, the teacher comes to the problem of making the lesson personal enough for the learners to see how the spiritual truth would operate in an actual life situation. The teacher must plan to secure the carry-over, for the lesson must not end simply in "talk" if it is to be effective.

A Comprehensive Lesson Plan

Undoubtedly the discriminating teacher has already asked the question, "How do the principles suggested in the preceding chapters fit together into a definite lesson plan?" Perhaps it would be helpful to the reader if some of the main ideas that have been presented are now lifted out and put together in outline form so that they may be seen as a whole. In working out a lesson plan the following matters should be kept in mind:

I. General Preparation
    1. The teacher's preparation of himself—in mind and spirit
       (1) Through Bible study
       (2) Through prayer
       (3) Through meditation—What has this truth (in the lesson to be taught) meant to me in my personal experience?
    2. What am I to teach?
       (1) Study carefully the suggested Scripture passage including the larger lesson
       (2) Use commentaries and other lesson helps
    3. Whom am I to teach?
       (1) General information concerning class members
       (2) Specific information concerning class members
          a What need or needs do my class members have that are met by this lesson?
          b What interests do my class members have that I can use to stimulate interest in the study of this lesson?

II. A LESSON PLAN
  1. What is my aim for the quarter?
  2. What is my aim for this unit?
  3. What is my aim for this lesson?
     (1) A good aim ought to be:
        a Brief enough to be remembered
        b Clear enough to be written down
        c Specific enough to be attainable
     (2) What kind of aim do I desire?
        a Do I desire a knowledge aim?
        b Do I desire an inspiration aim?
        c Do I desire a conduct response aim?
  4. How shall I secure purposeful Bible study? Do not read the Bible in the class until the class members have been stimulated and prepared to read it.
     (1) How shall I capture the interest of the group at the beginning of the lesson?
     (2) How shall I direct this interest toward a desire to read or study the Bible?
     (3) How shall I seek to insure that the reading of the Bible will be purposeful and meaningful?
     (4) What questions shall I ask the class in order to direct their study as they read the Scripture?
     (5) How shall I lead in the discussion of the questions after the Scripture has been read?
  5. How shall I develop the lesson so as to lead the class to accept and follow my aim for the lesson?
     (1) What suggested materials shall I use?
     (2) What suggested material will I have to leave out? (The aim that the teacher has in mind will determine this.)
     (3) What other material that is not suggested shall I use?
     (4) How shall I organize this material so that it will be in harmony with the needs and interests of my class members?
     (5) What questions shall I ask?
     (6) What problems shall I pose for the class to solve?
     (7) What method or methods shall I use?
  6. How shall I make this lesson personal?
     (1) How shall I lead the class to feel that this spiritual truth affects their lives today?
     (2) How shall I help them to see certain situations in their lives in which this spiritual truth would apply?

(3) How shall I lead them to the conviction that this truth is not only right but that they should follow it in practice?

7. How shall I secure carry-over?
   (1) How shall I seek to insure that what I teach will not die in the classroom?
      a Carry-over must be planned for.
      b Conclusions must be unhurried. Adequate time must be left for this part of the lesson.
      c It must be the class members' conclusions. Lead them to suggest ways for the carry-over.
   (2) What specific plans for this carry-over should be made?
   (3) What plan do I have to test whether or not any carry-over was made?

8. How shall I stimulate interest in the study of next Sunday's lesson?

A Simplified Lesson Plan

The lesson plan given above is too complex and cumbersome for a teacher to use each week. Therefore the following are given as simplified lesson plans. The teacher can easily keep them in mind as he prepares his lesson.

I. Lesson Plan for Conduct Response Aim
   1. Aim for quarter (or unit):

   2. Lesson aim:

   3. Securing purposeful Bible study:
      (1) To secure interest:

      (2) Transition

      (3) What to look for or to note as Bible is read:

   4. Developing the lesson: (Use only that material which will contribute to the achieving of your aim.)

5. Making the lesson personal:

6. Securing carry-over: (Be specific—lead to definite plans.)

II. LESSON PLAN FOR KNOWLEDGE AIM
    1. Scripture to be studied:

    2. Specific knowledge to be taught (outline major facts):

    3. Stimulating interest:

    4. Studying the Scriptures:

    5. Review of major ideas:

    6. Assignments for next week:

    7. Work to be done on project for quarter:

III. LESSON PLAN FOR INSPIRATION AIM
     1. Aim for quarter (or unit):

     2. Aim for lesson:

     3. Secure attention and interest:

     4. Developing the lesson:

     5. Conclusion:

These lesson plans may be reproduced in mimeograph form for teachers to use in their group study in the Weekly Officers and Teachers' meetings or in their private study. If it is reproduced on legal size paper the teachers will have sufficient space to make detailed notes.

The teacher might well ask, "How much time should be allotted to each division of this lesson plan?" That will vary, sometimes greatly, according to the lesson that is being taught. However, for the purposes of guidance the following is suggested:

Securing purposeful Bible study—6 minutes
Developing the lesson—12 minutes
Making the lesson personal—7 minutes
Securing carry-over—5 minutes

These suggestions are made on the assumption that the teacher will have thirty full minutes for teaching. However, at each point, the time suggested is all too limited. Take the matter of making the lesson personal. When the teacher gives the life situation and the class members become keenly interested in the problem under consideration, they usually have a discussion back and forth. The teacher will find that seven minutes is all too short a time to lead the group to re-accept the aim he is trying to teach.

CAN THE TEACHER ACHIEVE MORE THAN ONE AIM IN A LESSON?

In an earlier chapter it was stated that it would be unwise for a teacher to have an inspiration, knowledge, and conduct response aim in the same lesson. It was also suggested that, after these principles were discussed, the writer would try to point out why that was true. If the teacher has become aware of the vast amount of time that is necessary to lead the class members to the point where they understand the relation of a spiritual truth to their personal lives and then to the place where they are willing to practice that spiritual truth, the teacher will understand that there is certainly not enough time in one lesson period to do more than secure a conduct response. Of course, in securing a conduct response, a certain amount of knowledge is taught. But the knowledge is that which will lead the class members to accept and follow the spiritual truth under consideration. It is not a systematic study of Bible knowledge such as would be necessary to lead the individual to have a comprehensive knowledge of the Bible.

The teacher will also face the fact that when he spends some time leading the class to master a significant portion of Bible knowledge, he will not have enough time to secure a conduct response. What has happened too often in the past is that the teacher has tried to accomplish all three of these aims in one lesson; as a result, none of them was fully achieved. The approach that the teacher has to follow in teaching Bible knowledge and the approach that has to be followed in securing conduct response are so different that they cannot be adequately accomplished in one lesson. Therefore the teacher must face the fact that if he is going to secure results in the realm of either Bible knowledge or of conduct response, he must determine ahead of time which aim he desires and stick to that one with singleness of purpose. Only in this way can definite, concrete, observable, and measurable results be obtained.

Suggested Materials for Teachers

1. One volume commentaries

   Jamieson, Fausset, and Brown, *Commentary on the Whole Bible*. Price, $7.95.

   Dummelow, *The One Volume Bible Commentary*. Price, $5.00.

   Eiselen, Lewis, and Downey, *The Abingdon Commentary*. Price, $7.50.

   There is also a two volume commentary that is excellent:

   Alleman and Flack, *Old Testament Commentary*. Price, $6.00.

   Alleman, *New Testament Commentary*. Price, $4.50.

2. Bible dictionaries

   Miller, *Harper's Bible Dictionary*. Price, $7.95.

   Davis, revised by Gehman, *The Westminster Dictionary of the Bible*. Price, $5.00.

   Hasting's Dictionary of the Bible. Price, $10.00.

3. Bible concordances

   Cruden's Complete Concordance. Price, $3.50.

   Young's Analytical Concordance to the Bible. Price, $10.00.

4. Bible Atlas

   Westminster Historical Atlas to the Bible. Price, $6.00.

XII

TESTING OUR TEACHING

One means of teaching which has not been fully appreciated or adequately utilized by Christian teachers is through the use of various types of testing. Churches generally have been rather hesitant to use any form of testing for several reasons. Many felt they were dealing in areas that could not be tested adequately. Then, too, suitable tests were not always available, and it was difficult for an individual teacher or group of teachers to make up their own test. Perhaps the majority were hesitant because they were afraid that church people, children and adults alike, would resent any attempt to use any form of testing.

Recognizing the difficulties involved, it is still our opinion that properly used testing can become for the Christian teacher a very valuable tool in the teaching-learning process. In the first place, it may be used to stimulate the learner to have a deeper interest in learning. In the Uniform Lesson Series there is a quarter's study on the life of Jesus in the Gospel of John. On the Sunday before this particular quarter began, a simple Bible knowledge test was given to all the young people and adults in a certain Sunday school in the South. There were approximately 500 who took the test. Its purpose was to stimulate an interest in the study of the Gospel of John by leading them to discover how much they knew and how much they did not know.

It should be confessed that this undertaking was entered into with some fear and trepidation because nothing of this sort had ever been done in the church before. However, the fears were unfounded. The response was most enthusiastic, both among the teachers and the members. The teachers said that during the quarter their members studied their Bibles with greater diligence and entered into the class discussion with greater zest than they had ever done before. The response from the members was equally encouraging. One person seemed to sum up the feeling of the entire group when he said "Taking this Bible knowledge test stimulated my interest in studying the Bible more than anything I have ever done. We ought to have a test of this type at the beginning of every quarter to show us what we don't know."

In the second place, testing may be used by the teacher to determine whether or not he has achieved his purposes. Dr. Doak S. Campbell, president of Florida State University, relates the facetious story of a hunter who was telling a group what a thrilling and enjoyable experience he had shooting deer. When someone asked him how many he killed, he replied, "I don't know. I aimed and shot at seven, but I didn't take the trouble to find out whether I killed any or not." [1] Too often the teaching done in Sunday school is like that. The teacher does not bother to find out whether or not he has reached his objective.

There is no learning unless change takes place in the life of the individual. If a boy touches a hot stove a second time and is burned, we say, "You didn't learn your lesson the first time, did you?" He may have known that the stove was hot, but no change was made in the way he acted. Thus, no learning had taken place. The teacher needs to know whether change has taken place in the lives of his class members in order to know whether he has done any teaching. Of course, many of the most important outcomes of religious education cannot be measured accurately. Nevertheless, the teacher must undertake to evaluate the progress of his members in

[1] Campbell, Doak S., *When Do Teachers Teach* (Nashville: The Sunday School Board of the Southern Baptist Convention, 1935), p. 100. Used by permission.

those areas where it is possible and to the extent that it is possible.

Teaching Is Inevitably Tested

Someone has said that testing is simply "refined observation," for people are constantly testing by observation. A person may say he likes one automobile better than another. He means that he has observed the performance of the two automobiles and has come to the conclusion that one is superior to the other. He has not conducted any scientific test to serve as the basis of his conclusion; he has merely come to his decision through observation. When an individual says one boy is taller than another boy, or this girl is prettier than that girl, he too is testing.

So the question that faces the Sunday school teacher is not if his teaching will be tested or not, but, rather, how will his teaching be tested. The teaching will inevitably be tested. It may be left to chance or may be done more scientifically. Shall it be left to unreliable observation, or shall it be done more accurately?

Life tests one's teaching.—There may be those who feel that we should not have any type of testing in the Sunday school on the basis that it would make the Sunday school too much like public school and the members would resent it. Others feel that the matters we deal with in Sunday school are both personal and spiritual and any effort to evaluate or measure their progress would be sacrilegious.

Such attitudes are understandable but not convincing. The ultimate objective of the teacher is to teach for Christian living, and he needs to know if the member is becoming more Christian in his attitude and conduct. Is he increasingly becoming a better steward of his life, of his talents, of his time? Is he courageous in his stand for Christ, in his work for Christ? Life is the most rigid of all tests in teaching and is the one test which neither the teacher nor the learner can avoid.

Other people test one's teaching.—Other people observe the lives of the class members and evaluate one's success as a teacher. For example, someone may say, "Mr. Brown must be a marvelous teacher. He has taken that class of fourteen-year-old boys and done wonders with them." Again, testing is inescapable.

Class members test one's teaching.—Many teachers might be surprised to hear their class members' comments about them. Some would be very high in their praise. Other comments might not be so good. Whatever the comments may be, the teaching is being tested.

The final test of teaching.—In the final analysis, God tests the teacher's teaching. "Brethren, be not many teachers, knowing that we shall have the more severe judgment" (James 3:1, marginal reading). This is not given to frighten the teacher but to lead him to realize something of the seriousness of the task he has undertaken. He must understand that God expects—indeed, demands—more than mere lip service and superficial effort from those who teach in his name. God does not speak idle words, and when he says teachers will receive the more severe judgment, he means exactly what he says. The person who joins with God in the sacred task of teaching must have counted the cost and must be willing to pay the price of being an effective instrument in God's hand, both as regards what to teach and how to teach. The best way of teaching is all too poor. A poor way of teaching is sinful. And God is the final tester.

Various Types of Tests

When testing is mentioned to a group of Sunday school teachers, they almost immediately think of the tests and examinations that they had in the public school and usually rebel against any idea of testing in Sunday school. It must be remembered that the tests suggested here are not at all the public school type. People rather enjoy asking and answering Bible and religious questions. Various age groups often play a game called "Bible baseball" in which Bible questions are asked and the individual is required to answer the question if he is to get a "hit." Recently, the writer played a game with a group of adults in which they were required to identify certain Bible characters on the basis of statements that were given. The entire group of adults was fascinated by the game. Actually, it was a test of one's Bible knowledge. Now the question is, can tests be devised which evaluate the individual's religious progress but, at the same time, not have the unpleasant aspects of the old-fashioned type of examination? It has been demonstrated that they can be devised in the form of objective tests. Different types of objective tests are as follows:

1. *True-false test.*
   Mark "T" or "F" before the following statements indicating whether they are true or false:
   _____Jesus was born in Jerusalem.
   _____Paul was one of the 12 disciples.
   _____Judas was the disciple who betrayed Jesus.

2. *Completion tests.*
   Fill in the following blanks with the correct word or phrase:
   (1) The disciple who denied Jesus three times was _____.
   (2) Jesus was baptized in the River _____.

3. *Matching questions.*
   Below are some statements and a list of names to whom the statements apply. Put the number of the name in the appropriate space:
   _____He was the forerunner of Jesus.
   _____He was one of the sons of Zebedee.
   _____He led his brother to Jesus.
   _____Jesus first saw him under a fig tree.
   _____He was a tax collector whom Jesus called.
   _____He came to Jesus for an interview by night.
   1. Nathaniel
   2. Nicodemus
   3. James
   4. Andrew
   5. John the Baptist
   6. Matthew

4. *Multiple-choice questions.*
   In the following check the answer which correctly completes
   the sentence:
   (1) The Jewish temple was in
   _____Nazareth
   _____Jerusalem
   _____Bethlehem

   (2) Jesus was baptized when he was
   _____12 years old
   _____30 years old
   _____33 years old

If these tests are properly prepared, and if the teacher will
take the time to prepare the class for taking them, the class
will not resent them but will welcome the opportunity to
take them. This is true of adults as well as of children. This
type of testing can be done in any size church or in any community. In one small rural church, the teacher has been giving Bible knowledge tests to her Junior class for years.

Areas in Which Testing May Be Done

A teacher may not be primarily interested in his class
learning facts, but in their learning how to live the Christian
life. If so, Bible knowledge is not the only area in which the
teacher should try to test his teaching. He ought to include
at least the following areas: Bible knowledge, comprehension; attitudes, ideals, appreciations; choices, conduct and
character.

Examples of the types of questions that might be used in
these different areas are given below:

I. *Bible knowledge*—To see whether the members have a mastery of the facts of the Bible.
   Mark "True" or "False."
   1. _____The Jews and the Samaritans were friendly neigh-
      bors.
   2. _____Four of the twelve disciples of Jesus were Mat-
      thew, Mark, Luke, John.

Check the correct answer.
1. Jesus performed his first miracle at a wedding in
    _____Bethlehem
    _____Cana
    _____Nazareth
    _____Capernaum
2. The man who came to see Jesus by night was
    _____Zaccheus
    _____Philip
    _____Matthew
    _____Nicodemus

II. *Comprehension tests*—To see if the class members understand what the information they possess means.
    1. "Love your enemies" means
        (1) _____We should not harm our enemies.
        (2) _____We should do what our enemies want us to do.
        (3) _____We should help those who do us an injustice.
    2. To pray "in the name of Jesus" means
        (1) _____that if we say "in Jesus' name" God will give us what we ask.
        (2) _____that if we say "in Jesus' name" we have a better chance of getting what we ask.
        (3) _____that if we say "in Jesus' name" we are standing in Jesus' stead as we pray.
    3. "In honor preferring one another" means
        (1) _____We are to like those who like us.
        (2) _____We should not fight to get first place in the lunch line.
        (3) _____We should not have to take care of our little brother if we don't want to.

III. *Attitudes tests*—This is an exceedingly important area of testing for the teacher.

Since one of his major tasks is to lead his members to have and to follow Christian attitudes, he needs to know what their present attitudes are. Professor Frank McKibben suggests the following as an example: [2]

[2] McKibben, Frank M., *Improving Religious Education Through Supervision.* Printed for The Leadership Publishing Association by The Methodist Book Concern, 1931, p. 197.

"Would you be willing—

"(1) To go to the same church with

a French child	Yes_____	No_____
a German child	Yes_____	No_____
a Mexican child	Yes_____	No_____
a Japanese child	Yes_____	No_____
an Italian child	Yes_____	No_____
a Negro child	Yes_____	No_____

"(2) To live on the same street with

a French child	Yes_____	No_____
a German child	Yes_____	No_____
a Mexican child	Yes_____	No_____
a Japanese child	Yes_____	No_____
an Italian child	Yes_____	No_____
a Negro child	Yes_____	No_____

"(3) To go to the same school with

a French child	Yes_____	No_____
a German child	Yes_____	No_____
a Mexican child	Yes_____	No_____
a Japanese child	Yes_____	No_____
an Italian child	Yes_____	No_____
a Negro child	Yes_____	No_____

Another suggestion comes from Dr. Gaines S. Dobbins.[3]

"Check in the blank space to the left the three statements that best represent your viewpoint concerning Jesus Christ:

_____Jesus is my Saviour and Lord.

_____Jesus is the Saviour of all who repent and believe.

_____Jesus is the divine Son of God.

_____Jesus is the greatest teacher who ever lived.

_____Jesus shows us the way to live.

_____The most important thing about Jesus is not who he was but what he taught."

Choice test.—In this test, the teacher seeks to determine what choices the members have made in light of a given study. Again Dr. Dobbins gives a suggestion: [4]

[3] Dobbins, Gaines S., *The Improvement of Teaching in the Sunday School* (Nashville: The Sunday School Board of the Southern Baptist Convention, 1943), p. 158. Used by permission.

[4] *Ibid.,* p. 159.

"Check in the blank space to the left at least three choices that you have definitely made in the light of your understanding of the claims of Christ:

_____I choose Christ as the Lord of my life.

_____I sincerely turn from sin to a life of Christian faith.

_____I desire to follow Christ in baptism.

_____I want to win others to Christ and his church.

_____I am resolved to read my Bible and pray daily.

_____I wish to take some place of active service for Christ.

_____I propose to practice the principle of stewardship tithing.

_____For the present I prefer to be "a secret disciple."

_____I cannot give much time to Christian service.

Conduct and character tests.—The best way to test conduct and character is through the observation of an individual's daily life. Since it will not be possible for the teacher to do this adequately, he must often rely upon the observation made by the parents. The reader should refer to the section in the next chapter under the heading "Quarterly Parent Interview."

THE NEED FOR ACCURATE TESTING

The teacher may feel that his class will resent any kind of testing. But the need for *accurate* testing is so overwhelmingly acute that the teacher cannot afford not to test.

The seriousness of the task demands accurate testing.— Teachers of religion are charged with a most serious responsibility. They are not dealing with mere facts or figures, or with mere names or places. They are dealing with eternal truths as they are related to eternal destinies. Teaching in this area cannot be left to chance. It has already been pointed out that too many teachers today seemingly nourish the vague hope that some future good will come from their teaching, and there are some instances when the results may not be seen for years. However, the average teacher needs to know in the here and now how much difference his teaching is making in the lives of those whom he teaches. The task is too serious and the responsibility is too great to rely upon a vague hope that the right results will develop in the future.

The startling lack of Bible knowledge demands more accurate testing.—It is amazing as well as tragic how little the average person actually knows about the Bible even though he may have attended Sunday school for years. One writer tells of a Bible-knowledge test given to eighty-one tenth- and eleventh-grade high school students in a Southern town.[5] Nearly all of these students were regular attendants at Sunday school. The questions in the Bible-knowledge tests were purely factual, such as, "Who was the first man?" "Name the first five books of the Bible." "Who wrote most of the Psalms?" "Name the Four Gospels." The average grade was 35 per cent! Yet this fact was unknown until some tests were given. The teachers vaguely assumed that, because the class members were exposed to a certain amount of Bible knowledge, they were also learning it. Teachers must test their class to find out if the desired progress is being realized.

The need for improving teaching techniques demands accurate testing.—It is undoubtedly true that teachers for years have been using certain teaching techniques which have failed to achieve the desired intellectual and spiritual objectives. Yet they have had no way of determining whether one way of teaching was superior to another because they have had no system or plan for measurement or evaluation of the results.

One of the secrets of the almost unbelievable progress that has been made in industry in the last fifty years is the system of careful testing that has been devised and used. For example, in the automotive industry a carburetor is made and subjected to the most vigorous tests. Its weaknesses are discovered and experiments are performed until improvement is made. The scientists discover what will stand up under hard wear and what won't. They do not hold on to a procedure because it is the one they have always used. Through

[5] *Ibid.,* p. 153.

Testing Our Teaching 177

testing and experimentation, they are constantly finding ways of improving their product.

This is no attempt to equate human personality and machines. A human personality is alive. He has a will of his own. He cannot be placed in a test tube. But a type of testing and experimentation can and should be conducted in the area of Christian teaching to determine whether the techniques being used are effective, how effective they are, and to discover still better ways of achieving our spiritual objectives.

XIII

SECURING CHURCH-HOME CO-OPERATION

One of the most hopeful signs on the horizon today in religious education is the growing emphasis on church-home co-operation. Typical of the statements being made by leaders in this area is the following: "The family is primary in God's economy. It is the most potent influence in the development of personality. It may be the most effective means of Christian education. Nowhere else may religion be taught so easily and with such abiding results as in the home." [1] This emphasis must be encouraged. It must also be guided. At this stage of our progress we are able to see only "through a glass darkly."

There are many difficulties involved, many problems that must be solved. But solve them we must if our religious instruction is ever to approach the effectiveness we desire. *The church cannot accomplish the task of religious education alone.* That may seem like a shocking and extreme statement to some; nevertheless, it is true. The sooner church leaders and parents face this fact the better it will be.

One of the major problems confronting us in providing adequate religious instruction is the limited time available. Merely to point out that the church has the child only for a brief time on one week-day is to indicate the problem. In this

[1] Vieth, Paul H., *The Church and Christian Education* (St. Louis: Bethany Press, 1947), p. 168. Used by permission.

brief time teachers are supposed to give the individual the religious instruction that will enable him to develop Christian character. The task is too important and too complex to be achieved so simply and so briefly. This is not to minimize the place and importance of the Sunday school, nor to say that it cannot or has not made significant contributions to the spiritual development of multitudes of people. The Sunday school simply cannot and should not be expected to carry out the task of religious education alone.

The home also must accept willingly and intelligently its responsibility for the religious instruction of its children. There is ample evidence in the Bible and throughout Christian history to indicate that the home should be a—perhaps *the*—central agency in the religious training of children. "And these words, which I command thee this day, shall be in thine heart: And thou shalt teach them diligently unto thy children, and thou shalt talk of them when thou sittest in thine house, and when thou walkest by the way, and when thou liest down, and when thou risest up" (Deut. 6:6–7). During the Reformation the home was emphasized as a basic agency for religious training. Martin Luther was particularly strong in his statements as to the responsibility of parents in training their children. Said he, "Believe me, it is far more important that you exercise care in training your children than that you seek indulgences, say many prayers, go much to church, or make many vows." [2]

After the beginning of the Sunday school movement, the church leaders came to see in it an excellent opportunity for Bible teaching. They had high hopes of what it could accomplish. The church said, in effect, to the parents, "Send us your children and we will provide religious instruction for them." The parents were only too glad to shift the responsibility for religious instruction from their shoulders to the shoulders of the church. Through years of experience and

[2] Quoted in Seeley, Levi, *History of Education* (New York: American Book Company, Rev. ed., 1904), p. 167. Used by permission.

research, we have learned what we should have known all along: The church cannot accomplish that task alone. Now it is the responsibility of the church to recognize its limitations and to lead the parents to re-accept the share of responsibility for the religious education of their children which is rightfully theirs. This may not be easy to bring about, because the parents may be reluctant to assume this difficult task. However, the church must lead the parents to understand that they cannot escape the responsibility whether they want to or not. The church can supplement the work of the home, but it cannot take the place of the home in religious instruction.

Reasons for the Centrality of the Home in Religious Education

There is a growing appreciation of the importance of the home in religious education for, at least, the following reasons:

The home has the child during the most impressionable years of life.—Psychologists have been saying for years that the child's basic personality and emotional responses are determined in the very earliest years of life. They also tell us that even before the child is able to talk, parents, by their attitude and actions, by the very spirit and atmosphere of the home, begin to teach him their concepts of God, of prayer, of worship, of life. In these, the most impressionable and significant years, the child's religious development must begin. This must not be limited to a once-a-week affair, helpful as that will be.

The home has the child over an extended period of time.—One of the significant facts about the human species is his long period of infancy and his great dependence on parents. The child is subject to the authority and direction of his parents until the latter years of adolescence. In the child's infancy the home is practically the only influence in his life. During his pre-school age his horizon extends to include a few close friends in the immediate neighborhood of the home. When the child starts to school his world again expands. In middle adolescence, with the developing boy-girl relationships, his world extends even further. But, in all these stages, the home is still the dominant factor and the final authority in his life. The child's attitudes, ideals, and values are most profoundly influenced by his parents.

In the home, teaching is done in normal life situations.— One of the difficulties that has plagued Sunday school teachers is the fact that the teaching is done in classroom situations rather than in normal life situations. The teacher may try ever so hard to teach his class of ten-year-old boys the Christian ideal of forgiving others. But later in the week, when Johnny throws a rock at Bobby, he does not remember the Sunday school teaching at all; instead he takes after Johnny with both fists flying. He may have been able to quote the memory verse perfectly and answer all of the questions correctly, but he may not have seen any relation between the teaching in the classroom and this situation in daily life. However, the mother may come into this normal life situation and help Bobby to evaluate the situation in terms of the Christian ideal. Thus, parents have a unique opportunity to help the child understand the relation between religion and their normal life situations.

The home offers opportunity for repeated teaching.—This repeated teaching is essential to make a given attitude or a given course of action habitual. The teacher should not deceive himself into thinking that because the pupil has learned to state the proper Christian response that he will follow it in life. Neither should the teacher be deceived into thinking that just because the individual follows the Christian response once the action will become habitual. But, in the home, these normal life situations occur over and over again, and the parents have an opportunity for repeated teaching. In this way there is a much better chance of a given attitude or a given course of action becoming permanent in the life of the individual.

The home offers opportunity to observe results.—Another difficulty that the teacher often faces is providing opportunities to observe the results, if any, of his teaching. The teacher has little opportunity to see the class members in their daily life. In the home, parents have ample opportunity to observe their children's conduct and to know whether they are becoming more forgiving, or more thoughtful, or more kind, or more helpful. In the home, they can easily tell whether their children have "learned the lesson" or not. There, the test of learning is not answering a question but is life itself.

In the home the child learns by observation of other members of the family, especially of parents.—In many homes there is a picture on the wall of a child walking in the footsteps of his father. A significant truth is told by this picture. The child inevitably learns merely by being a member of the family. As Yeaxlee says,

The inescapable contribution which all parents make to the religious development of their children is wholly independent of whether a child is or is not "taught" anything whatever, either at home or at school or at church, if by teaching we mean, as we ordinarily do, the direct impartation of knowledge in the intellectual sense, or the practice of even such simple observances as saying prayers at bedtime and grace at meals. . . . For the issue here is not one of creed and observance, but one of character and daily relationships. In short, it is what parents are in themselves and how they behave that matters.[3]

From birth, the child unconsciously begins to develop attitudes which are similar to those of his parents. The four-year-old who comes to Sunday school and says, "I don't believe in foreign missions" is merely repeating what he has heard a parent say. These points of view quickly develop into attitudes.

Many child psychologists hold that the mother exerts the most influence in the life of the child, while others contend that the father has the most influence. It is probably deter-

[3] Yeaxlee, Basil, *Religion and the Growing Mind* (Greenwich: Seabury Press, 3rd ed., 1952), pp. 179–180.

mined by the one with whom the child most completely identifies himself. It is unquestionably true that both parents have a great influence. Children also learn from brothers and sisters, particularly older brothers and sisters. Thus, the home becomes a veritable school in which learning goes on all of the time. Members of the family are teaching when they are not aware of it, and children are learning when they are not aware of it.

In the home there is variety of experiences.—The experiences in the home cover all areas of the life of the child. In the Sunday school the teacher may not be too aware of the child's school life. Or he may not be aware of the child's attitude toward the underprivileged. But the home touches every area of the child's life. The home has the opportunity to interpret the significance of religion for one's school life, for one's studies, for one's recreational life, for one's friendships. Religion taught in and through the home would touch every area, every relationship of the child's experience.

The home is the source of authority.—During the latter part of the last century the home was a place of strict authority and rigid discipline. The father ruled with an iron hand. As a reaction to this stern concept of the home, a school of psychology came to the fore emphasizing the importance of freedom for the child. The family was to be a democracy. The child was to be given freedom to express himself so that he would not develop frustrations and neuroses. Although there was some value in this emphasis, it went to the extreme. Freedom for the child came to mean unbridled freedom.

Today there is a growing trend to place greater authority again in the home. This authority is balanced by the concept of the family as a democracy, but authority is again in the home. As the source of final authority, parents determine the sphere within which the child may develop his life and personality.

There is within the child a desire for family approval.— One of the basic needs of man is to feel wanted or to have a sense of belonging. No matter how much a child may rebel on occasions, there is a basic desire within him to have the approval of his family. This desire for approval will lead him to develop certain attitudes and to follow certain courses of action; it will even lead him to make certain sacrifices. Parents have a marvelous opportunity for teaching religion as they utilize this desire of the child for the approval of his family.

In the home parents have time to deal with the child as an individual.—In the Sunday school the teacher may complain, "How can I adapt this particular lesson to each different individual in my class?" Or "Johnny has a problem, but I simply do not have the time to help him." This is a natural difficulty which every teacher faces. In the home, however, the child is an individual of significance. It is true that parents are busy, but they should never be too busy to deal with their children as individuals. They may be trying to teach the children the religious attitude "Be ye kind." Mary may need one emphasis; Johnny may need an entirely different one. The parent has the opportunity to make the application of the spiritual teaching for each child. This is essential in good teaching.

THE OBJECTION THAT PARENTS CAN'T TEACH RELIGION

When the matter of home-church co-operation is discussed, the objection is often made that parents are not qualified to teach their children religion. There are three brief answers to this objection.

First, if the objection is true, it stands as an indictment of the teaching that has been done and is being done in our Sunday schools. Many parents have been in Sunday school for five, ten, or more years. If they have not become qualified to teach religion to their children, what have they been learning? If we are not teaching religion to our young people and young adults in such a way that they will be able to pass it on to their children, then perhaps we had better have a frank and fearless restudy and re-evaluation of the kind of Sunday school teaching that is now being done.

Second, the objection is not valid because the parents are teaching religion regardless. They may not be doing an acceptable job of it, but they are inevitably teaching it. Indeed, parents who never darken the doors of a church teach religion. Inescapably, inevitably, in the normal course of life, parents pass on to their children their attitude toward God, toward Christ, toward religion, toward the church. According to Yeaxlee, "Every parent has a part in the religious education of his or her children which must be played and is played, willy-nilly, consciously or otherwise." [4] Vieth states the same point of view in these words, "The reality and quality of religion are constantly tested within the home. Concealment is difficult and often impossible. Life changing influence is inevitable. . . . Is religion something which is merely professed, or is it lived? Before the child can frame the question, he knows the answer." [5] Thus, it is not a question of whether or not parents can teach religion; it is rather a question of what type of religion are they teaching and how well are they teaching it.

Third, if the objection is valid, then it is the responsibility of the church to revise its program of religious education in such a way that Christian parents will be better equipped for the task of giving religious instruction to their children. What better service can a church render than to lead young parents to build a Christian home and teach to religiously educate their children? Here is an area in which some serious study needs to be made.

THE DIRECT AND INDIRECT APPROACH

In this connection there is a rather fundamental problem that must be faced. The problem is centered around the question, "How is religion best taught in the home?" There are at least two points of view relative to this question. For want of a better designation we are calling them the direct and the

---

[4] *Ibid.,* p. 178.
[5] Vieth, Paul H., *op. cit.,* p. 169.

indirect approach. One view emphasizes direct instruction in the home through such means as daily family Bible reading and prayer, expressing thanks at meals, studying the Sunday school lessons with the children, planned or incidental conversations about religious matters, and so forth. The other approach holds that the most lasting and effective teaching is not done verbally at all, but is done indirectly through family relationships. So that, in the final analysis, it is not so important what is taught verbally but the matters of greatest importance are the kind of atmosphere in the home and the kind of relationships the child experiences in the home.

Those who accept the more direct approach emphasize the type of parent instruction that would enable the parent to co-operate more fully and more successfully with the Sunday school. That is, they would study material related to the Sunday school curriculum and would have as their problem the way it could be taught in various (even incidental) ways in the home. Fallaw seems to be following this point of view when he suggests that "the main objective of the church . . . should be to find out with parents where their limitations lie in their responsibility as religious teachers in the home, and to plan with them how to correct these limitations." [6]

Those who follow the more indirect approach emphasize the matter of making the home, in its totality, more Christian. This group is not so concerned with the Sunday school material the children are studying or with parental efforts to teach religion to the children directly. They would lead parents to be more concerned with a problem such as, "What does the Christian gospel mean to me and how is this gospel to be expressed in the relationships in the home?" Horace Bushnell expressed this view over one hundred years ago.

And if the parents desire better things for the child, as they probably say, the more guilty are they that, knowing and desiring better things, they thwarted their desires by their own evil life.

[6] Fallaw, Wesner, *The Modern Parent and the Teaching Church* (New York: Macmillan Company, 1946), p. 72.

Here then is the sin of Christian parents, that they try to make up by lecturing, teaching, discipline, for their mischief of a loose and neglectful life. Parents! Understand that it is the family spirit, the organic life of the house, the silent power of everyday godliness in the home, that influences your child toward God —or the lack of it that leads them away from God. If this godly spirit in the home in its everyday relationships be lacking, anything else you may do may almost be likened to trying to divert the flow of a mighty stream with a twig.[7]

Although Paul Vieth would not be identified with an extreme interpretation of either approach, he does point out the importance of having curricula materials designed especially for parents in helping them in the task they face. Since almost all denominations have accepted the point of view that what goes on in the home is as important for religious education as what goes on in the church, he says,

It would be natural to expect that if this were true, the curriculum-making bodies would take into account what should happen in both places; that these bodies would produce outlines for materials to be used in the home as in the church; that the training processes would reach parents as often as they serve church school teachers; that denominational publishers would provide as rich a variety of printed materials for family use as for the church school; and that the field forces of the churches would be skilled and concerned to improve the work of religious education in the home as in the church. . . . This is not the case. From the services rendered the local church, one would suppose that these agencies limit Christian education almost wholly to what is done within the church. Curricula are planned for use within the church, and suggestions and supplemental materials for the home are largely in the nature of making the *church* [emphasis his] curriculum more effective.[8]

Personally, I cannot accept the extreme of either of these approaches, but I see elements of value in both. On one hand, I would not want the family to have a formal, weekly session for the children in the home in which they were taught "re-

[7] Bushnell, Horace, *Christian Nurture* (New Haven: Yale University Press, 1947), p. 98.
[8] Vieth, Paul H., *op. cit.*, p. 181.

ligion." Neither would I want any family to depend on verbalizations alone in seeking to develop Christian character in the lives of their children. On the other hand, while there is real merit in learning through relationships, it seems to me that on occasions it is absolutely necessary to verbalize and interpret family relationships in terms of the Christian gospel. Otherwise, the child, in his thinking and understanding, may never get beyond the immediate family relationships to their counterpart, the Divine relationship. It seems that aspects of both approaches are essential to any effective program of parent education.

Plans for Church-Home Co-operation

Although much has been written concerning the need, even the necessity, for home co-operation, few plans have been suggested that a church might follow. In an effort to be as practical as possible we will suggest several possible plans. Plans of varying degrees of difficulty and complexity will be given.

Whether one adheres to the direct or the indirect approach in home instruction, or perhaps seeks to utilize elements of both, will influence whether one will accept or reject some of the following plans. It will also influence how one implements the plans he accepts. It must be recognized that, due to differing cultural and educational backgrounds, the degree of parental interest, and other factors, what would work well in one church might fail miserably in another. For this reason, the type of parental co-operation to be sought and the plan to be followed must be determined by the situation in any given church. It should also be stated that a church is not limited to following any one plan. It is likely that some churches will use several approaches at the same time. The order in which the following plans are given is of no particular significance.

The annual parent night.—This is probably the easiest plan for a church to follow. In it, parents who have children in a given department in the Sunday school meet on some night during the week with the teachers and officers of that department. Let us say, for example, the superintendent and other officers and teachers of a Junior department plan to have a parents' night. Since this meeting is held only once a year, it is probable that the best time to have it would be during the first or second week in October just after the annual promotion day. The teachers and officers invite all of the parents and their children to attend this meeting. The program might be as follows:

6:30–6:45 P.M.—Department superintendent in charge
Brief Scripture reading and prayer
Introduction of department officers and teachers
Presentation of general department plans for year

6:45–7:15 P.M.—During this period the children go with their respective teachers to their regular Sunday school classrooms. The parents remain with the department officers in the departmental assembly room.
1. The children and teachers
   (1) Have their class organization and the election of class officers
   (2) Make plans for future work
2. The parents and officers of the department, under the leadership of the superintendent, may be having a program such as:
   (1) What I expect of the Sunday school (given by a parent)
   (2) What the Sunday school expects of the parent (given by a department officer)
   (3) Ways parents can help. Here the department superintendent might give to the parents mimeographed sheets on which are listed the suggestions which the parents should follow in aiding in the Sunday school work. There could be a consideration of such items as why it is important for the child to be regular in

attendance, why it is important for the child to be on time, how the parent can help the child in the preparation of the lesson for Sunday, discussion of objectives, and so on.

3. General discussion in which parents ask and have answered questions in which they are interested.

7:15–7:30 P.M.—General session.

The children and teachers join the parents and officers in a general session. At this time each class can introduce the officers that have been elected, and one class might present a brief program.

7:30–8:30 P.M.—Social period.

A good social should have been planned in which the children, parents, teachers, and officers all may have fellowship together.

This plan is sufficiently simple and easy for any church of any size to follow. It requires only a group of officers and teachers who are interested in home co-operation to make plans for such a meeting. The above program would be applicable to all age groups. The officers and teachers could easily make whatever adaptations were needed.

The quarterly parent night.—This plan has very definite advantages over the one presented above. Since this meeting will be held once a quarter, the parents and teachers are able to discuss together matters relating more specifically to the teaching objectives. A suggested program follows:

6:30–6:40 P.M.—General worship period.

All children, parents, teachers and department officers meet together. One of the classes might have charge of the worship program.

6:40–7:00 P.M.—Planning period.

1. The children may go to their respective classes with their teachers to (1) evaluate the work of the past quarter, and (2) make plans for next quarter.

   2. During this period the parents and the department officers have a discussion of any general problems the department has and discuss future plans.

7:00–8:00 P.M.—Divided emphasis.

   1. Children: A social period is planned for the children under competent supervision.

   2. Parents: During this period the parents meet with the teacher of their child in the teacher's classroom. In this meeting the teacher may discuss with the parents the aims or objectives that he has in mind to teach for the next quarter. For example, the teacher may tell the parents that his aim for the first four Sundays is to lead the members of his class to become more helpful members of the family. For the next three weeks, his aim might be to lead the class members to render some unselfish service in the community. His aim for the next four weeks might be to lead the group to deepen their devotional life by practicing daily Bible reading and prayer. His aim for the other two Sundays might be to lead his class to be more reverent in the church.

It probably would be helpful for the teacher to have typed or mimeographed copies of these objectives and the dates they are to be studied. The parents can then discuss with the teacher whether these objectives need to be revised in any way, in what respects their children have needs in these areas, and how they may supplement at home the work of the teacher. Certainly, it will be beneficial for the parent to know that on a given Sunday his child is studying a certain Christian attitude. If the parent observes a lack of that attitude in the life of his child during the week, he will be able to supplement the work that has been done on Sunday. With parents and teachers both knowing and seeking the same Christian objectives, there is a better chance of leading the child to achieve these Christian ideals in life. The parents will come to have a much higher appreciation of the work of the Sunday school when they become aware of what the teachers are undertaking to do for their children. These two plans follow the direct approach in church-parent-child relationships.

The teacher's monthly visit in the home.—This monthly visit by the teacher is often made in addition to some of the other plans suggested here. Or, in some churches there may not be sufficient parental interest to have a special parent meeting. If this is the case, the monthly visit may be the major link between the home and the church. This plan necessitates, of course, small classes. Otherwise, too great a burden is placed on the teacher. In making the visit, the teacher should take with him (or her) the denominational magazine for the home. (Southern Baptists have *Home Life*.) The teacher chats about the work of the church and the Sunday school, the objectives he (or she) is trying to reach and other matters of mutual interest.

It is possible also during these visits for the teacher to emphasize the place of parents in religious instruction, the need for church-home co-operation and perhaps in this way stimulate concern on their part that may lead to a vigorous and vital program of parent education and co-operation. If necessary, assistant teachers may assist the regular teachers in this visitation. However, it should be pointed out that the regular teacher needs this personal contact with every home in order to understand the home background of each child.

A monthly parent information sheet.—This is another simple plan that may be used if active parent co-operation cannot be secured, or it may be used to stimulate parental interest. The major responsibility for this plan rests upon the church staff. This parent information sheet is mimeographed monthly and mailed to all parents who have children in the Sunday school. The church staff is responsible for determining the content of the sheet. It could deal with any and all matters that have relevance for children, parents, and religion. By discussing the child's religious development, by considering problems parents face, and by emphasizing that parents inevitably teach religion, it is entirely possible that parents might become sufficiently concerned to request more specific help.

Special parent institute.—For those churches that feel they would like to undertake a concentrated emphasis in this area, a special parents' institute is suggested. This institute may meet every night for one week or it may meet once a week for six to eight weeks or longer, according to the desire of the group. The problem here is, with all the matters that parents need to study, which ones will be selected for consideration during this brief period? The need and interest of the group will be the guiding factor in determining the course of study. It might include such matters as: How can I understand my child better? At what age can the child begin to understand certain religious concepts? What is my own theology; does it need clarifying? What does "learning through relationships" mean? How can I interpret the Christian gospel meaningfully to my child? A special institute of this type may lead to a regular weekly or monthly parents' class. This plan follows the indirect approach.

Monthly parent night.—Such a meeting might be designed to fit into either the direct or the indirect approach. Parents might meet with the teachers and discuss the lessons that are to be taught the following month and consider how they could co-operate at home. Or the parents might omit the consideration of the Sunday school curricula materials altogether and concentrate on problems relative to the development of their own spiritual lives and how they can interpret the gospel in their relationships with their children. This, really, is only a modified form of a parents' class that meets monthly rather than weekly.

The quarterly parent interview.[9]—In this plan, the teacher will have studied in advance the lessons for the next quarter

[9] This is an adaptation of the plan devised by Ernest M. Ligon in his Character Research Project. For a full explanation of his program see, Ligon, E. M., *A Greater Generation.*

and worked out his unit aims. He will state these aims in terms of Christian attitudes or Christian responses. The teacher will then work out a rating scale for each attitude. For example, one unit aim of the teacher might be, to lead each class member to develop a cheerful spirit when things are not going well. A rating scale for this attitude going from lowest to highest might be as follows:

1. Often moody. Thinks everyone is against him.
2. Gets angry easily when he can't have his own way.
3. Cheerful as long as things are going well.
4. Cheerful in almost all circumstances. Things rarely get him down.
5. Always cheerful. He has learned to take disappointments well.

Perhaps a second attitude the teacher might want to teach is to lead each class member to grow in his willingness to do assigned work well. The rating scale might be as follows:

1. Resents doing simple tasks at home and simple assignments at school.
2. Willing to perform simple tasks but not those which require much time, thought, and skill.
3. Whether he is willing or reluctant to accept work is determined by his mood of the moment.
4. Readily accepts tasks but shows some lack of persistence in finishing them.
5. Cheerfully accepts work as a necessary part of life and receives satisfaction from doing his work well.

The teacher, having worked out his aims in terms of attitudes and the rating scale on the attitudes, visits the parents of each of his class members. With them, he goes over the attitudes that he is going to try to teach for the next quarter. The teacher then asks the parents for information concerning how the child rates with regard to these attitudes. The parents are requested whenever possible to give specific illustrations of their child's attitude. This is absolutely necessary, because the teacher, in trying to help the child develop a more Christian attitude, must begin where the child is. This will also make the adaptation of the lesson much more personal.

After teaching the lessons for the quarter, the teacher will make the same plans including the rating scale for the lessons for the next quarter. He will again visit the parents of each member in his class. In this second interview, the teacher will go over the attitudes that were taught last quarter and discover from the parents whether there has been an appreciable improvement in the child with regard to these attitudes. For example, has the child been more cheerful in the face of disappointments? Has he improved in his attitude toward doing assigned work? After having gone over the lessons for the last quarter the teacher will then go over with the parents the attitudes that have been planned to be taught the next quarter.

The teacher may feel that the parent will resent his asking for this information. However, experience along this line has indicated that, rather than resenting this attitude by the teachers, the parents have been most gratified that the teachers have been sufficiently interested in their children to take their work seriously and have responded generously and graciously. In fact, the response of the large majority of parents has been most enthusiastic.

A great amount of work is involved in this procedure. However, if the teacher is interested in securing results in the lives of those whom he teaches, he must be willing to pay the price in work to achieve those results. God has not given us an easy task. If the teacher is not getting results from his present approach to teaching, let him not complain unless he will willingly pay the price to follow a better way.

Special parent classes.—Perhaps one of the best ways to enable parents to become better able to give the religious instruction their children need is in a parents' class. Such a class may meet monthly or weekly. It probably would be best to have these classes at night in order that fathers might

also attend. It might be that these classes could be integrated
with the regular Training Union program on Sunday night.
The Training Union would be rendering a significant service
in providing training in this important area. The children,
of course, are enlisted in their appropriate unions. However,
each group will have to determine what time is best for them
to meet.

In planning a program of parent education it must be kept
in mind that parents have different needs. There are those
who are potential or expectant parents. There are those
parents who have infants in the home. Others have children
who are just starting to school. Still others have children who
are going through the difficult adjustment period of adolescence. All of these parents have different needs and in seeking to minister to them, these needs must be kept in mind.

One of the most important steps in devising a program of
parent education is to lead parents to understand and accept
their responsibility in the total framework of religious nurture designed to help their children develop Christian character. Therefore, it will probably be necessary to hold some
preliminary meetings in which their place and responsibility
in the religious nurture of their children is frankly discussed.
Fallaw suggests that it would be highly desirable if out of
such meetings, parents and teachers could come out with an
agreement similar to the following:

1. We have agreed that:
    (1) Parents are the real teachers of religion—verbally, by at-
        titude and act;
    (2) Church school teachers are helpers—the main job lies with
        parents;
    (3) The church school stands ready to point the way of our
        common task.
2. This means that:
    (1) The home and church must come together at stated inter-
        vals for study, planning, and taking on specific tasks;
    (2) The very minimum of getting together is once a month—
        at the regular staff conference at the church;

(3) Our study together involves (a) knowledge of content taught by grades on Sundays; (b) certain week-day helps by parents; (c) understanding individual children.

3. At our monthly meetings we should:
   (1) Select one or more Christian principles which often cause perplexity, confusion, or perhaps disharmony between home teaching (either silent or vocal) and church teaching;
   (2) Probe the religious imperatives of these misunderstood principles and seek mutual understanding and/or agreement between home and church;
   (3) Insure consistent teaching in the home and church;
   (4) Elevate adult understanding, conviction and faith to the level found in the spirit of Christ.

4. When we meet we should avoid:
   (1) Random expressions of views often heard in general discussion groups;
   (2) Being fearful of discovering and following the truth in Christ—no matter what the implications and the cost may be to us.[10]

When we come to resource materials for a parents' class, it must be remembered that whether one accepts as more valid the direct or the indirect approach will influence both the materials selected for study and the guidance given to parents. For those who follow the more direct approach their study will consist primarily of a consideration of the Sunday school materials their children are studying. Their problem will be how they can supplement and make meaningful this teaching in the home. In this plan, instead of meeting with the teachers each quarter, the parents will be studying each week (or each month) what the teacher is going to teach. They will plan possible ways of relating the teaching to the child's normal, everyday experiences.

For those who follow the more indirect approach, their concern will be with making the relationships in the home more Christian. They can use such resource materials as: Donald Maynard, *Your Home Can Be Christian;* R. C. Miller, *The Clue to Christian Education;* Wilfred and Frances Tyler, *The Challenge of Christian Parenthood;* Wilfred

[10] Fallaw, Wesner, *op. cit.,* p. 117. Used by permission.

and Frances Tyler, *The Little World of Home;* Grace Sloan Overton, *Living With Teeners;* W. P. Crouch, *Guidance For Christian Home Life;* J. Ellenwood, *Just and Durable Parents.*

However, guidance is not enough. Parents need to be empowered to do what they know they ought to do. Here, the grace of God becomes increasingly meaningful to them. As parents sustain personal relations with God, his grace empowers them and they, in turn, become channels of grace for their children. In this way, parents truly become workers together with God.

XIV

THE WEEKLY OFFICERS AND TEACHERS' MEETING

Teachers readily admit their need for improvement. Most of them sincerely desire more training. But they are volunteer lay workers; they are busy people. They have other heavy responsibilities that demand time and attention. They have to make a living; they have a home to look after. As busy as they are, how can they get the training they need and want?

A person does not have time to do everything. Everyone must make a choice as to what he will do with his time. If he does this, he will not have time to do that. If he goes here, he cannot go there. No attempt will be made here to try to inspire the teacher to give more time to training. That is a choice the teacher will have to make. If the task of teaching the living Word of God to human beings is worth doing at all, it is worthy of one's best. There are literally thousands of busy people who are finding time to do God's work well. True, they have found that they do not have time to engage in many other activities. Many of them have given up some perfectly good and wholesome activities, clubs, and other engagements because they felt that doing God's work was more important. They have given up these things not in any spirit of sacrifice but because they have found more genuine joy and lasting happiness in doing the latter. Each person has just twenty-four hours in every day. It is his choice as to how he will spend them. He may use them for God, or he may use them for himself.

There are several opportunities for training open to the industrious teacher. He may take advantage of the special weeks of study using the approved denominational training course books. There are excellent books providing guidance in the study of the Bible, doctrines, principles of teaching, administration, and specialized activities. There is often held a city-wide or an associational training school with capable leadership in specialized areas. In addition to these special weeks of study the teacher may utilize the plan of home study. Denominational assemblies, on a statewide or denomination-wide basis, offer a wonderful opportunity for both inspiration and information.

All of these plans are good, and the teacher should make use of them. However, the suggestion being made here is that the best single plan for helping teachers improve their teaching is to use the weekly officers and teachers' meeting as a continuous school for teacher improvement.

WHAT IT IS

The weekly officers and teachers' meeting is a meeting of all the officers and teachers of the entire Sunday school. Those who work with all age groups are included. The meeting is usually held on Wednesday night immediately before prayer meeting. Perhaps the best way to explain what this meeting is would be to indicate the various divisions of it and give a brief explanation of each division.

Different churches use different plans and different schedules for this meeting. The plan and schedule that is probably most widely used is as follows:

6:00–6:30 p.m.—Supper (if desired)
6:30–6:45 p.m.—General Promotional Period (General Sunday School Superintendent in charge)
6:45–7:00 p.m.—Departmental Promotional Period (Departmental Superintendent in charge)
7:00–7:30 p.m.—Departmental Teaching Improvement Period (Group study leader in charge)

The meal.—The meal, of course, is optional. Many churches find that to have a meal makes it possible for more of the workers to attend. In many instances, the husband gets off from work so late it would be impossible for either the husband or the wife to come if they had to wait for him to come home for his meal and then return to church. Often, the husband meets his wife and children at the church for their evening meal. Let it be said with emphasis that if the church does provide a meal, it should be a *good* meal. These workers are giving freely of their time to the work of the church. They should not be asked to eat a tasteless, cold meal. One of the best ways to promote attendance is to have a delicious meal. This is not mundane or selfish on the part of the workers. After they work hard all day they should not be asked to come directly to the church to work another hour and a half and have only the usual type of church dinner. The workers may pay thirty-five to fifty cents for the meal. The church can subsidize the rest. This is one of the most fruitful ways the church can use its money. The more teachers that are reached and trained the better work will be done. When better teaching is done, more people will be won to Christ and the lives of Christians will be deepened and enriched. This is an investment in Christian living that pays off in eternal dividends.

The general promotional period.—In the general promotional period the officers and teachers of all departments meet together with the general Sunday school superintendent in charge. Fifteen minutes is usually given to this portion of the meeting.

1. Under the leadership of the general superintendent they make plans for promoting the work of the Sunday school as a whole. They consider such matters as:
    (1) Organization
    (2) Enlargement
    (3) Visitation
    (4) Reaching absentees

(5) Enlisting new members

2. They check on the work the Sunday school is now do-ing.

(1) Study of records

(2) Note progress of the various departments

(3) Note strong and weak points. Decide on aspects that need special emphasis.

3. Special projects are discussed.

(1) Revival

(2) Special emphases such as stewardship, training courses, census, etc.

Not all of these matters are discussed each Wednesday night. Time limitations will not allow such discussion. However, in the course of several weeks all of these matters, and others, will be considered. To make this meeting truly helpful and effective demands careful planning in advance on the part of the person in charge. Successful meetings do not just happen; they have to be carefully planned.

The departmental promotional period.—Immediately following this general period the group divides, and the workers of each department meet together for their particular group. They usually meet in their own department room where their records and other materials are available. The department superintendent is in charge of this portion of the meeting. Fifteen minutes is allotted for this period. In this departmental promotional period, the department superintendent does the same type of work that the general superintendent does in the general meeting, only it is done on a department basis. (In those churches where the Sunday school is not graded on the department basis, the group stays together for the entire meeting. The promotional period and the study period are carried on with all officers and teachers in one group.)

1. Study records to evaluate work being done.

(1) A report of what each class is doing.

(2) Strong and weak points are noted.

      (3) Absentees are discussed and plans made for reaching them.

  2. Departmental problems are considered.

      (1) Plan to enlist prospects.

      (2) Sunday morning schedule.

      (3) The type of departmental worship program for Sunday morning.

      (4) Class organization.

      (5) Problems of discipline.

  3. Plans for future work.

The plans that were discussed in the general session are presented to the department and the workers determine how they can promote these plans in their department. For example, if the Sunday school has decided to enter a special visitation program to reach the unenlisted, each department will discuss how it will do its part in carrying out this emphasis. Or if the Sunday school is emphasizing stewardship or evangelism, the department workers consider how their department can best carry out this emphasis. It can readily be seen how much more effective Sunday school work could be if all the teachers and officers of each department were working diligently together on the same emphasis. This unity of purpose and of effort is sorely needed in our Sunday schools. The department superintendent is responsible for seeing that the entire Sunday school program is carried out by his workers. In the department meetings, general plans for the over-all program are made specific for the department, and the workers have the opportunity to consider the problems that are peculiar to their particular department.

The department teaching improvement period.—The first two periods of the weekly officers and teachers' meeting previously discussed are concerned primarily with improving the promotion and administration of the Sunday school. The department study period is concerned primarily with the educational quality of the work done in the Sunday school. This is a period of thirty minutes in which the teachers are guided in the study and preparation of the lesson for the next Sunday. The group study leader is in charge with a particular emphasis on the improvement of teaching. It is this thirty-minute period that we propose should be used as a continuous school for teacher training. How this may be done is discussed in detail later in this chapter.

WHY HAVE IT?

A large number of churches have a weekly officers and teachers' meeting, but the majority do not. Those who have it are already convinced of its value. Those who do not have one do not know the value of such a meeting from personal experience. Therefore, they often ask, "Why have a weekly teachers' meeting?" Some churches have no planned meeting at all. Others have a monthly workers' conference, which is fine as far as it goes. It just doesn't go far enough. There is urgent need for churches to have a weekly meeting of its Sunday school leadership. This is true for both promotional and educational reasons.

The task of the Sunday school is to reach all people possible for Bible study and development in the Christian life. This is a worthy objective that deserves, even demands, our most vigorous promotion. Unless we are willing to give the time and effort necessary to achieve this objective, we are merely deceiving ourselves with our talk about our concern for the lost and the unenlisted.

Plans have been devised whereby the unenlisted can be found and reached. But the best of plans will not work unless those who are responsible carry out those plans. In a large business, the sales manager may have devised excellent plans for promoting the sale of the product. However, these plans will be of no avail unless the sales manager has an opportunity to meet periodically with his salesmen to share with them the information and the enthusiasm necessary to carry out the sales program, to note places of weakness, and to make further plans for future work. In something of the same way, if the work of the Sunday school is to go forward properly, the general superintendent needs to meet with his officers and teachers. He needs to share with them the plans that have been made and lead them to carry out those plans.

Fortunately or unfortunately, Sunday school teachers are human and, being human, are subject to the weaknesses of the flesh. We are all more or less prone to be negligent unless we are stimulated to work. It is at this teachers and officers' meeting that a part of this stimulation is aroused.

Yet it is more than mere stimulation which teachers receive in this meeting. They get a spirit of confidence and optimism. Nothing succeeds like success. As teachers meet each week to discuss the work together, as they hear testimonies of the progress being made and of the victories being won, there develops in the lives of many of the teachers and officers a spirit that is truly amazing. They begin to give more of their time, of their thought, of themselves to the work of the Sunday school. This has been demonstrated in the experience of so many different teachers in so many different churches as to indicate that it can and will work in any size church, anywhere.

The weekly officers and teachers' meeting serves to unify and correlate the work of the Sunday school. It enables the workers of all the various age groups to work together with the same emphasis toward the same goal. When no such overall planning is done, when each department is left to shift for itself, usually little or no work is done. Whether the Sunday school is emphasizing stewardship, enlistment, or evangelism, it is much better for all groups to be informed and working toward the same goal.

The teachers and officers' meeting is so organized as to provide an opportunity for general planning as well as for specific planning. But by far the most important reason for having a weekly officers and teachers' meeting is not promotional but educational. Teachers need to come together for study each week because they teach each Sunday. The teacher might say, "I don't need to attend such a meeting in order to teach on Sunday. I can study the lesson by myself." That may be true, but if teachers desire to become better teachers, they can use the weekly teachers' meeting as a continuous school for teacher improvement.

WAYS IT MAY BE USED FOR TEACHER TRAINING

There are several different ways the thirty-minute study period of the officers and teachers' meeting may be used. Probably the most widely used procedure is to have someone to teach next Sunday's lesson. Certainly, this plan has some values. Many of the teachers do not have any other chance to hear the lesson taught and enjoy hearing it at the teachers' meeting. While this is a commendable desire, they need to be reminded that this meeting is not primarily for enjoyment but for study.

Other teachers say they are inspired by hearing someone else teach the lesson. This is undoubtedly true, but again teachers must be reminded that they receive inspiration from the prayer meeting which immediately follows this meeting and from sermons on Sunday. The teachers' meeting is not primarily for inspiration but for study. There are those who say they get ideas and information when they hear the lesson taught. This is important, but it is believed that more ideas and information can be gained through some other plan of study.

Another approach that is rather widely used is known as the "angle method." In this plan the teachers study the lesson from different angles. One teacher is asked to bring in one or more possible aims for the next Sunday's lesson. Another teacher is asked to come prepared to suggest a way to introduce the lesson. Still a third teacher is asked to give the major ideas that might be used in developing the lesson. Another "angle" is current events that might be related to the lesson. Someone else might prepare to show how they plan to secure participation by the class. Finally, another teacher comes prepared to indicate how the lesson might be specifically applied to life.

This approach has several good features. For one thing, it secures the active participation of the group. It provides an opportunity for the teachers to share their experiences with one another. It gives variety to the study period and helps keep the interest of the entire group. However, there is at least one serious disadvantage to this plan. It lacks unity. The various teachers present the different "angles" or parts of the lesson from their own particular point of view. One may have chosen to follow one emphasis in the lesson, while another may have chosen to approach the lesson in an entirely different manner. Thus at the close of the study period, the teachers do not have a comprehensive, unified view of the lesson. Nevertheless, in spite of this weakness this plan has been used rather effectively by many groups.

Teachers need training in areas other than methods of teaching. For this reason the study period of the weekly officers and teachers' meeting may be used for Bible study. This would be particularly fitting when the teachers decide in advance that they want to have a "knowledge aim" for a given quarter. If the lessons for the quarter are taken from a particular book in the Bible, or if they deal with a certain period of history, the teachers may decide that they want to make a serious, thorough, systematic study of the facts contained in that book or period. All teachers readily confess their need for this type of study. This is an approach that needs to be used more. The effectiveness of such a study will largely depend upon the person chosen to lead it. As suggested in an earlier chapter, the teachers may thus be helped to clarify their own theology and the theology they are teaching their classes.

The final plan suggested here is to use this period to study educational principles with supervised practice in preparing next Sunday's lesson. This seems to present the best possibility of any approach thus far considered. This plan will be explained in detail in the next section.

Let this word be said here. None of these programs of study should be used to the exclusion of all the others. For example, the group may desire to spend three months studying educational principles. The next three months they may want to concentrate on Bible study. It is best to keep variety in this study period of the weekly officers and teachers' meetings in order to keep the interest alive.

A Continuous School for Teacher Training

As suggested above, perhaps the best plan yet devised to give teachers the guidance they need in improving their teaching is to use the study period to present briefly some educational principle or teaching technique and then give them an opportunity to "practice" using it as they prepare the lesson for next Sunday. The thing that will prove most helpful in this approach is the idea of providing practice for the teachers in using a given principle under the supervision of a leader. The plan works somewhat as follows. First, the leader of the study group, together with the teachers, works out a course of study they desire to follow. They might use the educational principles suggested in this book as a guide. They could use one of the books on teaching in the denominational leadership series. Each Wednesday night the leader introduces the educational principle that is to be considered for that night. This would have to be done as briefly as possible to allow time for practice in using the principle in preparing the lesson.

For example, if the group were studying "How to make the lesson aim specific," the leader would make a brief explanation of this topic. The teachers would then undertake to work out a specific aim on the lesson they are to teach next Sunday. The leader would help each teacher to evaluate and revise his aim in the light of his presentation, and they would proceed to prepare the rest of the lesson. The group probably should spend several weeks on a problem such as "aims."

This would be necessary for two reasons. The first is that sufficient time would have to be given for the teachers to have a thorough understanding of the principle being studied. The second is that the teachers should have a number of weeks in which to practice using the principle so that they will be able to apply it in preparing any lesson without the supervision of the leader. The idea behind this plan is not to see how many principles can be covered in a given amount of time but to stay with a principle until the teachers know how to use it.

Let us suppose that the teachers are studying the problem "How to introduce the lesson so as to secure a purposeful study of the Bible." The leader would make a brief presentation of this topic and, perhaps, give an example or two. The teachers would undertake to apply the ideas suggested as they prepared their lesson. After the teachers had worked on the lesson for a while, the leader would ask each teacher how he planned to introduce the lesson and would help each teacher to evaluate his work. Was the introduction in line with the interest of the group? Was it in line with the aim of the lesson? Each teacher would benefit by the leader's discussion with every other teacher. They would then prepare the rest of the lesson together.

It can readily be seen that this primarily is a *study* group with each teacher actively participating. It is highly important that the group be small enough for each teacher to get individual attention from the leader. Unfortunately, there are some superintendents and teachers who feel that they cannot have a good meeting unless they have a large group. But when we are teaching skills, as we are doing in helping our teachers to know how to teach, it is even more important that each one has individual attention. It is probable that from five to eight persons make the best number for a study group. If there are as many as fifteen to eighteen teachers in a department, it would be wise to make two or three study groups. Otherwise, some of the teachers will be "lost" in the group, and they are usually the ones who are in need of the most help.

A variation of this plan has also been used with success. In this approach, the leader selected the major divisions in a lesson plan as the course of study, namely:

1. How to make an aim specific
2. How to secure purposeful Bible study
3. How to develop the lesson
4. How to make the lesson personal
5. How to secure carry-over

He spent five successive nights with the teachers discussing each of these topics. The leader and the teachers then met each Wednesday night for three months and practiced working out these steps using the lesson for the following Sunday. The advantage of this variation is that it gives to the teachers a comprehensive view of the entire lesson plan at the beginning of the course of study. It was found that this introduction deepened the enthusiasm of the teachers for the course of study and also enabled them to learn to apply the principles more quickly. The teachers indicated that it helped them "to know where they were going."

The teachers who have followed this plan have found it best to sit around a table where they can write and talk together. Each teacher is provided with a mimeographed lesson plan sheet (cf. pp. 160 *ff.*). He determines whether he wants to have a knowledge, inspiration, or conduct response aim for the lesson and is given the appropriate lesson plan sheet. The group then studies the lesson, using the sheet as a guide. One thing should be made quite clear here. It is absolutely essential for the teachers to study the lesson before they come to the teachers' meeting. Otherwise, the study group will be merely a "pooling of ignorance." In planning the lesson, the leader does not do all of the talking. Each of the teachers shares his ideas and experiences. All during the discussion of the lesson the teachers are filling in their mimeographed lesson plan sheet with the ideas and suggestions they like and plan to use. At the close of the session each teacher has prepared for himself a rough outline of his lesson for Sunday. He has the rest of the week to revise and "polish" it for Sunday.

ADVANTAGES OF THIS PLAN

The plan of using the weekly teachers' meeting as a continuous school for teacher training has several advantages. First, it gives the teachers help in studying and preparing the lesson. Many times in the past, groups have taken ten to twelve Wednesday nights studying principles of teaching. The teachers have indicated that such a study was helpful, but they complained that while this was going on they missed getting the specific help they needed to teach the lesson for next Sunday. This plan avoids this difficulty by studying the lesson each week.

Second, in the past, when the teachers received help in studying the content of the lesson, they were given no guidance in ways to improve their teaching. This plan provides an opportunity for teachers to improve by studying principles of education and teaching techniques.

Third, this plan provides the teachers not only with the opportunity to study principles of teaching, but it also gives them the opportunity to practice using them in working out an actual lesson. It helps to take these educational principles out of the realm of the theoretical and makes them practical. It also helps to overcome one of the major weaknesses that has attended most efforts at teacher training. Usually, teachers have spent each night for one week studying teaching techniques. But the following week when they tried to prepare the lesson, they did not know how to apply the principles they had studied. Therefore, most teachers continued to prepare their lesson as though they had never taken the course of training. This is not altogether the teacher's fault.

What we seem to have overlooked in our plans for training our teachers is the fact that for a teacher to know an educational principle does not mean that he will know how to use it. To expose our teachers to these principles or even to lead them to the place where they have a thorough understanding of these principles does not at all imply that they will know how to apply them in the preparation of a lesson. Too often, in our efforts to train our teachers, we ourselves have fallen into one of the major pitfalls we have sought to lead our teachers to avoid—to assume that to know *what* automatically means to know *how*. The plan suggested here avoids that pitfall by providing an opportunity for the teacher to apply the principle as he plans a lesson under the supervision and guidance of the leader.

Fourth, this plan also has the advantage of utilizing the technique of "on the job training." The teachers are going to have to teach the lesson next Sunday and any help they can get is always appreciated. The teacher has an interest and a sense of need which is conducive to learning. Closely related to this is the fact that the principle being studied is not "stored up knowledge" for future use. They put it into practice immediately in preparing the lesson; they try it out in an actual situation on Sunday; and, on the following Wednesday night, they analyze and discuss the successes and failures they have realized.

Fifth, using the weekly officers and teachers' meeting as a continuous school reaches more teachers over a longer period of time than any other type of teacher training program. A weekly teachers' meeting is a regular and accepted part of the program in a large number of our churches. This will become increasingly true in the future. These churches are reaching a high percentage of their teaching staff every Wednesday night. The possibility of leading this vast number of teachers one night each week in improving their teaching, not for weeks or even months, but for years is indeed thrilling to contemplate. Training courses that last for one week are helpful. But obviously this does not provide the time needed for adequate training. The matter of teaching is a difficult undertaking. It cannot be learned quickly or easily. Thus, this opportunity to study and improve over an extended period of time is an absolute essential.

Finally, this plan has in it those principles which are conducive to learning: (1) The teachers have a sense of need —they have to teach the lesson for next Sunday. Any help is welcome. (2) They have an interest—they want to improve. They want to be better teachers. (3) They have an opportunity to learn through doing and not just listening. They apply what is being studied in preparing the lessons. (4) They have an opportunity to put into practice what they have just studied by using it in teaching on Sunday. (5) They have an opportunity for review and evaluation when they come together the following Wednesday night. At that time they review the experiences they had on Sunday to determine wherein they succeeded and wherein they did not succeed and why.

SOME QUESTIONS CONSIDERED

Perhaps the major question that arises in connection with following this plan is: Who is to lead the teachers in this study? This is an important question. The effectiveness of this procedure will largely depend upon the knowledge, insight, and ability of the leader in the area of teaching principles. Whether or not he has sufficient understanding of the principles of teaching and whether he has sufficient insight and ability to help the teachers evaluate their efforts to apply these principles will determine the measure of improvement. If the leader has no such insight, it will simply be a matter of the blind leading the blind. The leader must be one who has an understanding of the principles of teaching, one who has an understanding of the Bible, and one who has an understanding and appreciation of the spiritual objective of the Sunday school.

In many churches, the pastor may be the only one qualified to lead. He will probably have Seminary training and should have qualified himself in this area during his years of study.

It is recognized that the pastor is already overworked. Yet, it is probable that the pastor would do more good to a larger number of people by helping his teachers improve their teaching than he could by almost any other means. Jesus used this approach. He spoke to large groups, but his main area of concentration was to gather his small group of disciples about him and give them special training and instruction in the task they were to do. Actually, the pastor will be able to touch the lives of more people intimately through his teachers than he will through any other means. If he helps his teachers improve their teaching, if he enables them increasingly to get results in Christian living, he will be touching and blessing the lives of every person who comes to Sunday school.

If the church has a minister of education, he would be the logical one to be the leader of this group study. He is responsible not only for promoting and administering the educational program of the church, he is also responsible for lifting the educational level of the work that is done in the organizations of the church. Thus, one of his major tasks as well as one of his greatest opportunities is to be the teacher of his teachers.

In some churches, some other person might particularly be qualified for this task. It is essential that the church secure the services of the best qualified person to assume this responsibility, for it is likely that there is no more important task in the entire Sunday school than this.

The question may be raised, how can small departmental study groups as suggested earlier have adequate leadership for each of them? To be realistic, it should be recognized that in some cases it may be necessary for the leader to teach all of the teachers in the entire Sunday school. No one else is qualified. When this is the case, the teacher should try to give as much individual attention as possible. While this situation may be necessary in some churches, it is far from ideal. Another possibility would be for the leader to spend three months with each of the departments giving them guidance. Of course, while he is with one department, the other departments would have to get along as best they could (as they are doing now). The advantage of individual instruction would have to be weighed against this disadvantage.

The best solution to the problem would be to have each department elect an associate department superintendent in charge of training. This person would not teach a class on Sunday, but he must be eminently qualified to teach if he is to be the teacher of the teachers in his department. The qualified group leader—perhaps the minister of education— will get with these departmental associates and give them an intensive course of study on the principles of teaching. This course of study may be held on Sunday morning during Sunday school or on some week night. When it is to be held is determined by the group. How long it is to last is determined by the needs of the group, although it probably should last at least thirteen weeks.

The leader gives them the personalized instruction they are later to give their teachers. He helps them to learn to evaluate whether an aim is specific or not, whether the introduction is sufficiently interesting, whether a given method is properly used, etc. After this course of study is finished, these associate department superintendents then meet with the teachers in their departments each Wednesday night and lead them in their study of educational principles. The general group leader may visit the various departments to note the progress being made and to render assistance as needed. In order to help these departmental group leaders prepare for each Wednesday night and to give them additional guidance and practice in applying the educational principle being studied, the general group leader may continue to meet with them in a special class on Sunday morning at the regular Sunday school hour. They could study together the principle to be discussed on Wednesday night and then apply it to the lesson for the following Sunday. In this way the general group leader will be able to lend guidance each week to those who will be the group leaders on Wednesday night.

This plan is not fantastic or idealistic. It is workable and practical. It simply demands that we take seriously the task of helping our teachers. We will never have the type of teacher-training program we need, nor will we have the improved teaching we desire, until we are willing to dedicate both our time and our best leadership to it.

The Teaching Improvement Period Demonstrated

Perhaps it would be helpful if we were to try to give an example of how this study period of the weekly officers and teachers' meeting might be used to help the teachers understand and apply a teaching principle.

Background for demonstration.—A few words of explanation should be given to serve as a background for the demonstration which is to follow. We will say that we have been discussing the unit, "Helping the Teacher Understand What Teaching Is." Two Wednesday nights ago we had a discussion of "Transmissive Education." We saw that the primary aim of this type of teaching was the transmission of knowledge. In that period, we saw the advantages and limitations of this type of teaching. We found that, though knowledge was necessary, it was not the primary aim of Christian teaching. As we examined our teaching together, we found that we were merely "telling" our pupils rather than teaching them. All of us seemed to sense that something was lacking. We wanted to find a better way of teaching.

The next Wednesday night we discussed a different approach to teaching—"Creative Education." In this study, we saw the need for class participation rather than having the teacher do all the talking. We saw also that one of the functions of the teacher was to stimulate thinking on the part of the class members. Then we took last Sunday's lesson and prepared it with these two ideas in mind. Now we come to the demonstration.

The demonstration.—"You recall just before we left last Wednesday night, Mr. Jackson said he felt he just wasn't getting anywhere in his teaching. He said his class just came together, studied the lesson, agreed that the ideal was right, but they would go out and not do anything about it. He wanted to know how we could make our teaching more practical so that something would be done about what we teach. Mr. Jackson has hit upon a very important point. Do any of the rest of you feel as he said he felt?"

The leader should give an opportunity for the teachers to respond before continuing.

"Perhaps we could call our discussion tonight 'Teaching that leads to changes' or 'How to secure carry-over.' There are two or three things that we need to understand in connection with this idea of teaching for change."

The teacher would then lead the group in a brief discussion of this problem. He might use an outline similar to the following:

1. There is no real teaching unless changes take place. Where there is no change, there is no learning. Where there is no learning, there is no teaching.

2. This change can take place in several different areas, such as:

    (1) Increased knowledge
    (2) Changed attitudes
    (3) Heightened appreciation
    (4) Increased skills
    (5) Changed conduct

3. How to get this change? That is the question.

The change must be planned for in the preparation of the lesson. Too often a change is not obtained because it is not planned for. A lesson is taught but no definite plan is made to secure change or to get response on the part of the class members.

    (1) Exhorting is not enough.
    (2) In the preparation of the lesson the teacher should

ask himself these questions (they should be written on the blackboard as this constitutes the heart of what the leader is trying to get the teachers to follow):

a. What changes or responses would I like to see the members of my class make?

b. Can they begin doing this next week?

c. How can I lead them to see the need for making these or some other responses?

d. How can I lead the members to make their own application or suggest their own response?

e. How shall I lead each member (if possible) to a definite commitment without embarrassing any?

f. What plan will I have to see whether the responses were actually made?

After giving this introduction to the principle being considered, the teacher would then lead the teachers in the study of the lesson they are to teach on Sunday. It is here that he guides them in applying the principle already studied.

Let us say that the leader is working with a group of Junior teachers and that the lesson is found in James 1:22–25, 2:14–20. Let us see how the practice period would actually work out. The leader might use the following lesson plan:

1. Aim for the lesson:

When the leader asks for suggestions, Mrs. Brown gives the following, "To lead my class members to be doers of the word, and not hearers only." The leader would help her evaluate this aim: "Mrs. Brown, is this aim specific enough? You know if we want to get conduct response, we have to make our aims specific."

MRS. BROWN: "Oh yes, I remember our discussion on that topic. I just can't seem to get out of my old habit of thinking in broad, general terms. The aim I suggested is broad enough to cover the whole area of Christian experience. Is this better, 'To lead my class members to express in action one basic Christian teaching which they have not been following?'"

LEADER: "Yes, that is much better. Do you have a specific response in mind?"

MRS. BROWN: "Yes, in fact I have a different response in mind for each member of my class."

In this same manner the leader would lead each teacher to analyze and evaluate his aim and continue to guide them in their lesson preparation, using the following divisions:

2. Securing purposeful Bible study:
3. Developing the lesson:
4. Making the lesson personal:
5. Securing carry-over:

It is at this point that the leader would plan his greatest emphasis on this particular night because this is the point that is related to the discussion which the leader gave at the beginning of the session.

LEADER: "We now come to the part of our lesson planning that is related to the discussion we had at the beginning of our period tonight. We agreed that if we were going to get change in the lives of our members, we would have to plan specifically for it as we prepared our lesson. Now, how can we make plans for getting a response in this lesson? Let us look at the questions on the blackboard we are to keep in mind. The first one is, 'What changes or responses would I like to see the members of my class make?'"

MR. JACKSON: "I would like for the members of my class to be more consecrated."

LEADER: "That is certainly a worthy objective, Mr. Jackson, but is it not too general? What are some specific things that your members need to do that would be an expression of deeper consecration on their part? We need to make it specific enough that they can begin expressing it this week."

MR. JACKSON: "Well, one thing they need to do is to read the Bible more. I don't believe I have a single member who reads the Bible during the week."

LEADER: "Perhaps, then, the specific response you might seek is to lead them to begin reading their Bible daily."

MR. JACKSON: "That's certainly more specific than the general response I first suggested."

MRS. DUVALL: "I think the response my class needs most is to obey their parents better. In my conference with the parents last month we had quite a discussion of this problem."

(The leader would help each teacher evaluate his desired response. Some teachers might have one response for the entire class, others might have in mind a different response for each member.)

LEADER: "Another question we need to face is this: How can we lead our members to see the need for making some specific response?"

MR. GRAVES: "I plan to do this when I make the lesson personal by using a life situation."

MRS. BROWN: "I think I'll discuss with them the temptation we all face of just 'talking' about religion. At the close of our discussion I'll just ask them if they are willing to do more than just talk. Then I'll ask what they are willing to do."

LEADER: "Mrs. Brown has brought up the next question we need to consider. How can we lead our members to suggest their own application of the lesson?"

MRS. DUVALL: "I think I will ask them to suggest ways they can be 'doers of the word,' and list them on the blackboard."

MR. JACKSON and MR. GRAVES: "That's a good idea. I think I will do the same."

LEADER: "The next question is always difficult to answer. How can we lead our members to a definite commitment and yet not embarrass anyone?"

MR. GRAVES: "I'm just going to ask my boys to resolve to be better Christians this week."

LEADER: "I'm afraid, Mr. Graves, that experience has indicated that a general exhortation like that doesn't get much response. It's like the general exhortation we hear so often. 'Let's everybody bring someone with them to Sunday school next Sunday.' Unfortunately, we don't get much response Again, we'll have to be more specific."

MRS. DUVALL: "After I have my members list ways they can be 'doers of the word' and we discuss them, I'm going to ask them to select something that they are not now doing that they will begin doing next week. I'm even going to ask them to raise their hands when they have selected one."

MR. JACKSON: "I like your suggestion, but I don't believe I'll ask them to raise their hand. I fear that would put too much pressure on the group and might embarrass some."

MRS. DUVALL: "I know my girls well enough to know they wouldn't mind."

LEADER: "Of course, you teachers know your class best. Each class has to be handled differently, but we do have to be careful not to embarrass or put any type of pressure on our members. Now, what plan will we have to see whether the responses were actually made?"

MR. GRAVES: "You have me there. I don't have the slightest idea."

MR. JACKSON: "It seems to me that the following Sunday we could use the 'early time' before our department assembly to have an informal review of last Sunday's lesson. We could discuss what we did about it during the week—if anything."

MR. GRAVES: "Say, that's a good idea. You know, one of the reasons I like these weekly teachers' meetings so much is that we have an opportunity to share ideas. I could have gone the rest of the week and never would have thought of a way to check on the responses of my members."

LEADER: "Good for you, Mr. Graves. You have hit on one of the real values of this meeting. When teachers get alone at home, they find it is difficult to work out some of the points in our lesson plan. Often it is not easy to find a way to secure purposeful Bible study or to make the lesson personal. Studying the lesson alone the teacher often gets discouraged. In group study in teachers' meetings with everyone sharing their ideas, it's really fun. Well, how about you ladies, how are you going to check on response?"

MRS. BROWN: "We are having a class meeting at my home the following Friday. I think I'll bring it up there."

MRS. DUVALL: "This is quite a significant lesson for my class. They need it so deeply that I think I will have a personal conversation with each one sometime during the week."

LEADER: "That's fine. We have had a very profitable session tonight. Next Wednesday night at the beginning of our study period we will give each of you an opportunity to tell how you got along with your teaching on Sunday. We will see whether or not you feel this plan will help us get more results from our teaching."

We cannot afford to do Sunday school work in a half-hearted, haphazard way. Experience has indicated that a weekly meeting of the workers helps the Sunday school better to achieve its spiritual objectives. There will be many who will say they do not have time to attend a meeting of this type each week. There will be some who have valid reasons that make it impossible for them to attend. However, the large majority can come. Having the supper at the church solves many of the problems. Many who thought they were too busy have put this meeting into their weekly schedule and have been amazed at how quickly this became a part of their regular routine. Now attending the weekly officers and teachers' meeting is just as normal a part of their Sunday school life as attending on Sunday morning. Busy people can attend this weekly teachers' meeting; thousands are already doing it. And the work of God goes forward through the Sunday school, because they give this time for planning and study.

XV

THE IMPORTANCE
OF THE TEACHER

Over one thousand Sunday school teachers were asked the question, "What meant most to you in your Sunday school experience before you became a teacher?" Between 85 and 90 per cent of them replied, "A teacher." An educator tells of a similar group of Sunday school workers who were discussing their own experiences as pupils in the Sunday school. "It was decided that each was to name the most important influence that had come into his life. Without exception each named a person or persons and not abstract truths. One after another could point to some one teacher who, as a person, had done more toward shaping his life than had any other factor." [1] Think back over your own experience. Was this true in your case?

If the experiences of these teachers are typical of all those who attend Sunday school, then this fact has tremendous significance for teaching and learning. In considering the teaching-learning process great emphasis is always given to educational principles and teaching techniques. This emphasis is proper. But the experiences of these teachers would indicate that the single most important factor that influences learning is the *life and personality of the teacher*. This factor has not been sufficiently emphasized in the past.

[1] Vieth, Paul H., *How to Teach in the Church School* (Philadelphia: The Westminster Press, 1935), p. 26. Used by permission.

We have all heard it said, "What you are speaks so loudly I can't hear what you say." This is doubly true with a Christian teacher. The teacher teaches for good or ill largely because of what he is. His attitude toward God and life, his likes and dislikes, his prejudices, his very habits of speech and manner of dress are as inevitably a part of his teaching as any technical skills or methods.

The teacher seems to be a sort of stained glass window, and the sunshine of God's truth shining through the teacher's mind, spirit, and life takes on the glow and the color of that teacher, whether it be bright and glowing or whether it be dark and gloomy. Perhaps you have had the experience of going from the brilliant sunshine outdoors into some church; the moment you stepped inside you had a feeling of being depressed because it was so gloomy. At another time, you may have gone into a church and, as the sun streamed through the stained glass windows with its cheerful colors, it seemed as though God was truly present. What made the difference? The sunshine was the same. The difference in the color and appeal within the churches was determined by the stained glass windows through which God's sunshine passed. The same is true of Christian teachers. God's Word is the same. Sometimes, it is not as attractive and appealing as it might be. At other times, it glows with magnetic beauty. The difference is the teacher through whom the Word of God flows.

Teaching techniques and knowledge of content are of little use unless they are used by one through whose life the truth of God may flow in sincerity and purity. Eavey is eminently correct when he says, "The teacher may teach a little by what he says; he teaches more by what he does, but most by what he is." [2]

Christian truths are better understood when seen in life. God has revealed himself in nature. He revealed himself still more through the words of the prophets. But when he wanted

[2] Eavey, C. B., *Principles of Teaching for Christian Teachers* (Grand Rapids: Zondervan Publishing House, 1940), p. 79. Used by permission

to reveal himself and his truth completely and finally to the world, he did so through a Person—Jesus, his Son. What does it mean for a person to be devoted to Christ? What does it mean for a person to live a consecrated life? What does it mean for a person to live a life of faith? It is difficult to get a person to understand these spiritual concepts through the use of words alone. But they can be completely understood when the one who seeks after truth sees them demonstrated in a Christian's life.

In the same manner, lives are impressed and changed far more by truths they see demonstrated than by those they hear spoken. This brings up the problem of learning through identification. We learn best from teachers with whom we tend to identify ourselves. Perhaps, then, the basic need in our Sunday schools is for teachers whose life, whose personality, and whose Christian experience are such as will make the Christian life both desirable and attractive. Thus the place to begin the improvement of our teaching is with our teachers. When our teachers are the kind of teachers whose lives embody the truths that they seek to teach, we will not need to have fear for the results.

THE TEACHER MUST EXAMINE HIS CHRISTIAN EXPERIENCE

Basically, teaching is a sharing of experience. If this is true, that which the teacher should desire most of all to share is Christ. But the teacher must have a genuine personal experience with Christ, and he must have genuine experiences with Christ in other realms of life. The teacher must know something of temptation and the power of Christ to help overcome these temptations. Indeed, he must have had Christian experiences in all of the relationships of life, for he can share only those things that he himself has experienced. If the teacher simply is a parrot to repeat what is said in the lesson helps and has no experience in his own personal life, Jesus may ask of him, "Sayest thou this thing of thyself, or did others tell it thee of me?" (John 18:34.)

Sometimes, those who criticize modern religious education point out that in the early church they did not have a "program" of religious education. It may be that we have placed too great an emphasis on some of the externals of our "program." Perhaps we need to be called back to what must be the central emphasis in religious education. The Christians in the early church had an experience to share, and they shared it enthusiastically. This is the very heart of religious education.

A Plan for Self-Improvement

If the life and personality of the teacher is such an important factor in influencing the Christian development of those whom he teaches, then while he is trying to improve his teaching techniques, he also should try for self-improvement. Near the close of his public ministry Jesus prayed, "For their sakes I sanctify myself" (John 17:19). In that hour he was setting himself apart; he was concentrating upon himself. Yet this was not at all selfish. It was necessary, for in the final analysis what he must do for the world depended upon what he did and how he reacted in the situation which he was to face. Even so, the Christian teacher must concentrate upon himself. For the learner's sake, he must sanctify himself; he must set himself apart. For, in the final analysis, much of what he will be able to do for the Christian development of his members depends upon him—his life, his personality, his Christian experience.

If our teachers are to improve, they must have a plan for self-improvement. Improvement comes not by accident but by conscious effort. The plan must be carefully worked out, consciously entered into, and systematically followed.

The first step in devising such a plan would be to lead the teachers to make a list of what they consider to be the essential qualities of a good teacher. In working out this list, the teachers should be both idealistic and realistic. The probability is that they will major on generalized qualities. For example, someone will suggest that a good teacher ought to be consecrated. That is true, but "consecration" is such a broad, general term. How should this consecration be expressed in a specific way? In listing the qualities of a good teacher, be as practical and specific as possible. The following items might be suggestive for teachers as they make their list:

1. Be regular in attendance.
2. Be on time.
3. Begin preparation of the lesson at the first of the week.
4. Keep a notebook of information concerning the class members.
5. Visit in the home of each member at least once each month.
6. Attend the weekly officers and teachers' meeting.
7. Follow a systematic plan of Bible study.
8. Have personal, daily devotions.
9. Follow a definite plan for improving my teaching.
10. Have a growing Christian experience.

This list may be expanded by the teachers to include whatever qualities they may desire. They would perhaps want to consider certain physical qualities such as sound health, neat appearance, sufficient physical energy, good posture. Even more important are qualities of personality such as cheerfulness, emotional stability, friendliness, approachableness, sense of humor. Qualities of one's spiritual development are the most important of all, yet they are the most difficult to identify and evaluate: Is my relationship with God in Christ alive and growing? What am I doing to develop my spiritual life? What do I do outside of church to express my Christianity? Do I do more than "talk" about the evils in my community?

After the teachers have worked out the list of qualities that should be in a good teacher, it should be mimeographed in a form similar to the one shown on page 229 *f*. This mimeographed form should then be presented to them along with a challenge. and they should be led to adopt it as their plan for self-improvement. The teacher is to take this sheet home, and during his prayer time, alone with God, he should rate himself honestly and fairly on these qualities. The rating may be on a basis such as: excellent, very good, good, weak, poor. After he has rated himself, he should select the one point where he is weakest and work on that particular matter for one month. This is being systematic. Psychologists tell us that it is easier to concentrate on one weak point at a time than it is to try to concentrate on many in general.

At the end of the month, the teacher should go to his quiet place and check himself again as to the items on the rating sheet. If he has been working on the weak point of being on time, he looks back over the month and sees whether or not he has improved in this regard. He perhaps finds that he has improved in his weakest point. If so, then he changes his rating on that point from "poor" to "good" and selects his next weakest point as the one for him to work on for the coming month.

The probable reaction of the teacher to this suggested plan will be something like this: "This is very childish. I know I ought to do better and I'm really going to try to improve, but I don't need any silly little plan to help me." Admittedly the plan is simple. It was intended to be so. However, the real reason the teacher reacts against this plan is that it pins the teacher down closer than he likes to be pinned down. If he can just resolve in general to improve, in two or three weeks he will forget about it, and his resolution will not bother him. But if he works out this self-rating scale and, before God, resolves to improve, that little sheet will be a constant reminder to plague and condemn him until improvement is made. We had just as well face it, unless we have such a definite systematic plan, the likelihood is that we will not improve at all.

The Master Teacher said, "For their sakes I sanctify myself." For their sakes the Christian teacher must do likewise. There must be a *willingness* to improve on the part of each teacher. We must face this inescapable fact. *The one area—the teacher, his life, his spirit, his personality—that is the most important single influence in the learning process is the one area over which we have complete control.* We cannot control the lessons; we cannot control attendance; we cannot control the weather; but we can control and improve ourselves. The question is, are we willing to pay the price? We must consider the lives of those whom we teach; we must consider the God who saved us; we must consider the God-given task that has been entrusted to our keeping. We may rebel at following a systematic plan for self-improvement, but it will help us. It will bless those whom we teach, and God will smile with favor upon us.

CHECKING MYSELF AS A TEACHER

	Excellent	Very Good	Good	Fair	Poor
Regular in Attendance					
On Time					
Begin Preparation of Lesson the First of the Week					
Pupil Information Notebook					
Visit Each Member Once a Month					
Attend Weekly Officers and Teachers' Meeting					
Follow a Systematic Plan of Bible Study					
Daily Devotions					
Definite Plan for Improving My Teaching					
Growing Christian Experience					

THIS IS MY WEAKEST POINT
WITH GOD'S HELP I WILL IMPROVE

October_____   April_____

November_____   May_____

December_____   June_____

January_____   July_____

February_____   August_____

March_____   September_____

USING THE CHART TO IMPROVE

1. With the names on your class roll and this chart go to a quiet place to be alone with God.
2. Read each name and visualize each face.
3. Honestly and objectively go over each qualification and ask the question, How do I rate?
4. Look over the checks that have been put in the column marked "Poor," consider the weakest point, and resolve with God's help to work on this point all during the next month.
5. Ask God's help in becoming the kind of teacher your class needs and deserves.